THE
FLOW
OF THE
SPIRIT

*Divine Secrets of
a Real Christian Life*

JOHN G.
LAKE

W
WHITAKER
HOUSE

Unless otherwise indicated, all Scripture quotations are taken from the King James Version of the Holy Bible. Scripture quotations marked (ASV) are from the American Standard Edition of the Revised Version of the Holy Bible.

Notes to the Reader:
This book is not intended to provide medical advice or to take the place of medical advice and treatment from your personal physician or other qualified health care professionals. Neither the publisher nor the compiler nor the compiler's ministry takes any responsibility for any possible consequences from any action taken by any person reading or following the information in this book. If readers are taking prescription medications, they should consult with their physicians and not take themselves off prescribed medicines without proper medical supervision. Each reader is solely responsible for the consequences of his or her personal choice concerning consultation with physicians or other qualified health care professionals.

Several times in this text, John G. Lake used the words "colored," "native," and "Negro" in reference to mixed-race or black people to distinguish from whites. Such was the terminology of his day, and in no way was Lake expressing a prejudiced or racist attitude. We have chosen to leave his words as he originally stated them so that the reader could better understand the context of what Lake was communicating.

Words in boldface type in Scripture quotations indicate the emphasis of John G. Lake.

All word definitions are taken from the electronic version of *Merriam-Webster's 11th Collegiate Dictionary*, © 2003.

Definitions of Hebrew and Greek words marked (STRONG) are taken from electronic versions of *Strong's Exhaustive Concordance of the Bible*.

Material compiled by Roberts Liardon.

THE FLOW OF THE SPIRIT:
Divine Secrets of a Real Christian Life
(Previously published as *Living in God's Power*)

Robertsliardon.org
https://www.facebook.com/Robertsliardon/

ISBN: 978-1-64123-024-7 • eBook ISBN: 978-1-64123-029-2
Printed in the United States of America
© 2012, 2018 by Roberts Liardon

Whitaker House • 1030 Hunt Valley Circle • New Kensington, PA 15068
www.whitakerhouse.com

The Library of Congress has cataloged the original trade paperback edition as follows:
Lake, John G.
  Living in God's power / by John G. Lake ; compiled by Roberts Liardon.
    p. cm.
  ISBN 978-1-60374-436-2 (trade pbk. : alk. paper) 1. Spiritual formation. I. Liardon, Roberts. II. Title.
BV4511.L35 2012
252'.0994—dc23
                    2012014114

This book has been printed digitally and produced in a standard specification in order to ensure its continuing availability.

CONTENTS

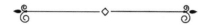

Part III: Life in Christ

Part IV: Sanctification and Consecration

WHY YOU SHOULD READ
JOHN G. LAKE

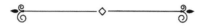

"No words of mine can convey to another soul the cry that was
in my heart and the flame of hatred for death and sickness that
the Spirit of God had stirred within me. The very wrath of
God seemed to possess my soul!"
—*John G. Lake*

T hese words summarized the passion that propelled the lifelong
ministry of John G. Lake (1870–1935). He spoke these words in reference to the intensity of emotion he felt as his thirty-four-year-old sister
lay dying. He had already witnessed eight of his fifteen siblings die from
illness; yet, he had also witnessed the miraculous healing of his own
childhood rheumatoid arthritis, as well as a sister's breast cancer and
a brother's blood disease, both under the ministry of John Alexander
Dowie. It was already too late to take this sister, who now lay at death's
door, to Dowie's Healing Home in Chicago, so he telegraphed Dowie
with a desperate plea for prayer. Dowie telegraphed back: "Hold on to
God. I am praying. She will live." That simple declaration caused Lake

to wage a furious spiritual attack on the power of death—and within the hour, his sister was completely healed.

It was battles such as this that brought John G. Lake face-to-face with his convictions. Was he going to stand by as the enemy took yet another loved one from him, or was he going to choose to stand in the enemy's way? Such an opportunity again presented itself on April 28, 1898, when his wife of five years lay dying. Jennie was battling for breath in her final hours when Lake finally put his foot down. He would not tolerate the enemy stealing away the mother of his children and his spiritual partner. He determined to believe God's Word as it was revealed to him for her healing. He contended for her life in prayer, and as a result, she rose up healed and praising the Lord in a loud voice. News of Jennie's miraculous healing spread, and from that time on, Lake was sought after for the power of his healing anointing.

John G. Lake is thought to have had the greatest healing ministry in the modern age. He reportedly raised several people from the dead, cast out demons, and ministered healing to people with cancer, missing eyes, and every imaginable kind of disorder.

As a wealthy businessman, Lake heard the call of God, sold all of his possessions, and moved with his wife and seven children to South Africa, where he served as a missionary for several years. His ministry was characterized by dramatic and powerful healings that gave a mighty witness to the Spirit of God.

After returning to the U.S., Lake set up Healing Rooms in Spokane, Washington, and Portland, Oregon, where over one hundred thousand people were documented to have been healed.

Today, there is a renewed interest in Lake's teachings, which cover every area of healing. Lake taught that any Christian should be able to heal the sick, saying, "All that is needed, is for the person praying…to let the tangible Spirit of God flow through them into the sick person."

John G. Lake had a remarkable ministry. His legacy includes not only his books and writings, but also a foundation of thought that played an important role in the early development of the Pentecostal movement and in the growing presence of divine healing in our world. He helps us understand that even ordinary believers can consecrate themselves to God and learn to minister the gifts of healing.

ABOUT JOHN G. LAKE

John Graham Lake was born on March 18, 1870, in St. Mary's, Ontario, Canada. His parents moved the family of sixteen children to Sault Ste. Marie, Michigan, while he was still a young child. At the age of twenty-one, he became a Methodist minister; however, he chose to start a newspaper in Harvey, Illinois, instead of accepting a church ministry. From the newspaper business, Lake expanded his career pursuits by opening a real estate office in Sault Ste. Marie when he and his young, ailing bride returned there for her health.

In 1901, at the age of thirty-one, Lake moved to Zion, Illinois, to study divine healing under John Alexander Dowie. In 1904, Lake decided to relocate to Chicago, buying himself a seat on the Chicago Board of Trade. Within a year's time, he was able to accumulate over $130,000 in the bank and real estate worth $90,000. This prompted the notice of top business executives, who asked Lake to form a trust of the nation's three largest insurance companies for a guaranteed salary of fifty thousand dollars a year. He was now a top consultant to business executives, making money through hearty commissions as well. By turn-of-the-century standards, John Lake was making a fortune.

During his business life, Lake had made it a practice of speaking somewhere practically every night, after which he joined like-minded friends in seeking the baptism in the Holy Spirit. Finally, in 1906, while he and another minister were praying for an invalid woman, he experienced profound "currents of power" rushing through his entire being, and the woman was instantaneously healed.

Such was the power of his anointing that he wrote about it as being like the lightning of Jesus: "You talk about the voltage from heaven and the power of God! Why, there is lightning in the soul of Jesus! The lightning of Jesus heals men by its flash! Sin dissolves and disease flees when the power of God approaches!" Lake would also compare the anointing of God's Spirit to the power of electricity. Just as men had learned the laws of electricity, Lake had discovered the laws of the Spirit. And, as God's "lightning rod," he would rise within God's calling to electrify the powers of darkness and solidify the body of Christ.

For a while, Lake was able to juggle his great secular success and his growing desire for God. He had learned to walk in the Spirit, noting: "It became easy for me to detach myself from the course of life, so that while my hands and mind were engaged in the common affairs of every day, my spirit maintained its attitude of communion with God." But by 1907, he yielded to the call to full-time ministry. He and Jennie disposed of their bank accounts and all real estate holdings by giving everything away to charity. From that point on, the Lakes relied on God alone for provision as they traveled the country ministering.

By January 1908, they began praying for the necessary finances to take their team to Africa. In April of that same year, the Lakes departed for Africa with only enough money to pay for passage on the ship. In faith, they believed God for the finances necessary to gain them admittance into the country and for provision once they arrived. The Lord provided exactly what they needed as they were lining up to pay the South African immigration fees in order to leave the ship. Before the family even left the dock, a miraculous housing offer presented itself and they immediately settled into a furnished home in Johannesburg.

Days later, John was asked to fill in for a South African pastor who was taking a leave of absence. Over five hundred members of the Zulu tribe were in attendance his first Sunday in the pulpit, and as a result, revival broke out to such an extent that, within weeks, multitudes in the surrounding area were saved, healed, and baptized in the Holy Spirit. The success astounded Lake so much that he wrote: "From the very start, it was as though a spiritual cyclone had struck." In less than a year, he had started one hundred churches.

Ministry success came at a price, however. Before the year was out, on December 22, 1908, Lake came home to find Jennie had died. He was devastated. Early in 1909, he returned to the States to recuperate, raise support, and recruit new workers. By January 1910, he was headed back to Africa in the midst of a raging plague there. He was among the few who ministered to the sick and dying. He proved to local physicians that the germs would not live on his body due to the Holy Spirit alive in him. He actually verified this under a microscope, showing that the germs died upon contact with his body. Those who witnessed the experiment stood in amazement as Lake gave glory to God, explaining: "It is the law of the Spirit of life in Christ Jesus. I believe that, just as long as I keep my soul in contact with the living God so that His Spirit is flowing into my soul and body, no germ will ever attach itself to me, for the Spirit of God will kill it."

In 1912, after five years of ministry in Africa, having produced 1,250 preachers, 625 congregations, and 100,000 converts, Lake returned to the United States. In 1913, he married Florence Switzer, with whom he had five children. They settled in Spokane, Washington, where they founded the Spokane Healing Home and Apostolic Church, which drew thousands from around the world for ministry and healing. In May 1920, the Lakes left Spokane for Portland, Oregon, where he started a similar apostolic church and healing ministry.

By 1924, Lake was known throughout America as a leading healing evangelist. He had established forty churches throughout the United States and Canada, in which there had been so many healings that his congregations nicknamed him "Dr." Lake.

In 1931, Lake returned to Spokane at the age of sixty-one. He was weak with fatigue and nearly blind. God ultimately restored his vision after Lake had a "talk" with the Lord about it. Then, after returning from a church picnic on Labor Day 1935, John G. Lake went home to be with the Lord. He was sixty-five years old.

Today, Lake's legacy is being rediscovered by Christians who long to experience Jesus's prophetic words: *"Verily, verily, I say unto you, He that believeth on me, the works that I do shall he do also; and greater works than these shall he do"* (John 14:12). Too often, it feels like this expression of Christian faith is a distant dream, reserved only for the most anointed men and women of God. As you read John G. Lake, keep in mind that he was no such idol, but merely an ordinary man who obeyed the voice of the Lord in radical and unprecedented ways. He was a normal man who laid it all down for the glorious gospel.

We are surrounded by a generation that seeks answers to difficult questions in a world that often seems to be spinning out of control. The fundamental foundations of human morality appear to be crumbling. The answer will be found as God raises up a generation of men and women who will radically obey God no matter the cost, as John G. Lake did in leaving his fortune for the sake of the gospel. The Lord is looking for men and women who will have the audacity to believe in dramatic moves of the Spirit, as Lake did when he demanded that plague cells be placed on his hand so all would be able to see the fire of God burn them up. God will use wild, faith-filled believers from every nation, tribe, and tongue in greater ways than He used John G. Lake. The revival that is coming will be ushered in through vessels who are faithful in the small things so that the power and presence of God will remain pure and sustained.

John G. Lake never said there would not be trials and difficulties, but the prize of being a son or daughter of God was Lake's aim for everyone to whom he ministered and dared to believe that the Word of God is true...all of it. When his faith took action, miracles took place. Let us ask God to anoint us with this same power as we believe in His callings for our lives.

PART I

SALVATION

1

THE REAL CHRISTIAN

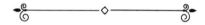

October 11, 1914
Spokane, Washington

When I first commenced to preach the gospel, at least after I got to the point where I gave up everything else and gave my life exclusively to the gospel, a number of my friends from the city of Chicago were in the habit of coming out to hear me preach, brokers from the Board of Trade and other business friends who were in my circle. It was sort of a curiosity. One day at the club, one inquired from a friend, "Have you heard Lake preach yet?"

He said, "Yes, last night."

And the other said, "How was it?"

"Well," he replied, "it was wonderfully apostolic. He took a text and went everywhere preaching the Word."

When the secretary inquired yesterday what the subject of my sermon would be, I told her it was "The Real Christian." I trust the Lord will let me keep in reasonable touch with the subject. However, I would rather the Lord would have His way than mine.

A Christian is unique. He stands alone. He supersedes all who have gone before. He will not have a successor. He is man at his best and God's best effort for mankind.

When the conception of a Christian has been established within our spirits as the New Testament establishes the ideal Christian, we will understand then how it is that men have been ready to abandon all else in the world in order to attain Christ, in order to attain His character, in order to become the possessors of His Spirit.

I went to South Africa in a most unique time in the nation's history, just after the reconstruction period following the Boer War. On account of the Great War, the native populace had been frightened practically out of the country. They had gone far back from the war zone, and the war zone covered practically the whole country.

The great mines were depending on the natives for labor, and it became a great issue as to how it would be possible to carry on the work while this condition of fear rested upon the natives. Finally, it was proposed that they should bring one hundred thousand men from China. They were brought on a contract for three years. The British government sent a fleet over to China and brought them all out at one time. They were a real living colony. They brought their teachers, preachers, priests, and prophets. Chinese are largely Confucians and Buddhists.

At the same period, the East Indian people who live in South Africa (and there are many of them; I think in the Transvaal alone there are two hundred and fifty thousand of them) felt that they were not receiving the attention from the government in the way of education that they ought to, so the British government sent teachers, both religious and secular, to supply them there.

So the Buddhist priests, the Yogis, and many others came and made their headquarters at Johannesburg. Our ministry was somewhat unique. We were the only ones who held [meetings] and preached on the subject of healing.

After a little time, it dawned on me that here was a possibility that had never come into my life before. If I could get these priests and teachers of the various Eastern religions to come together, we might have an exchange of thought. We would have something accomplished. It would at least give me an opportunity to discuss their beliefs. I was familiar to some extent with the Eastern religions, but I never had any touch with the soul life.

So, after some time, the matter was arranged. At the same time, we added to our company a rabbi from Chicago, Dr. Hearst. We had a combination, I presume, representing all the great religions on earth. We were able by wise exchange and guidance and much prayer to finally bring about such a condition of fellowship among these various ones that they spoke out their hearts to each other with a great deal of freedom. Many times we sat from sundown to sunup comparing notes and going over the various teachings, etc.

It had such an effect on me that I left that series with this conclusion: There is lots of light in the world, and men are groping after the light. Some possess it in a larger degree than others, but all possess it in some degree. I said to a man as I walked home on the last morning, "One thing surely has been demonstrated, and that is that in Jesus Christ there is a divine life of which, when a man becomes a real possessor, he has a richer appreciation of his power that no other man possesses." And I have been more of a Christian, of a real Christian, from that day than I ever was before.

I am convinced tonight that there is a profound secret in the life, character, teaching, and virtue of Jesus Christ that when a man attains it, he is rich indeed beyond measure.

In order to have you appreciate some of the things that I trust the Lord will let me say, I want to relate some incidents. It seems as if I can teach things through incidents that I am not able to teach in any other way.

Among my young friends in South Africa were two young men whom I have regarded as the brightest men I have ever known. One was a Boer. His name was Von Shield, the son of an old-line stock of highly educated Hollanders. The other's name was Kritzmall. He had come from a generation of Church of England preachers. I think his great-grandfather had occupied St. Paul Church in London. I believe he had been baptized there himself.

He has always stood out in my mind as a sort of counterpart of St. Paul, for if I can comprehend the character of Paul, I think he was more largely duplicated in that man than in any other I ever knew.

These two men were really the only up-to-date "new thought" men I met in Africa. Von Shield was an agent for Christian D. Larson and handled his books in South Africa. He began to attend our meetings and, one day when I was not present, came forward out of the audience and knelt at the altar and sought God for the conscious knowledge of his salvation. And, bless God, he received it.

Some days after that, when I was present, I was teaching at the afternoon service on the subject of the baptism of the Spirit. Raising up in his seat, he said to me, "Lake, do you suppose that if God gave me the baptism of the Holy Spirit, it would satisfy the burning yearning that is in my soul for God?"

I said, "My son, I don't know that it would, but I think you would be a long piece on the way."

So, without more ado, he came forward and knelt, and, looking up, he said to me, "Lay your hands on my head and pray." As I did, the Spirit of God descended on Von Shield in an unusual manner. He was baptized in the Holy Ghost very wonderfully, indeed. He was a transformed man, I tell you. From that hour, that man became the living personification of the power of God, and in all my life I have never found a soul through whom such majestic, intense flashes of power would come as through his soul at intervals. He was not a student of the Word of God. Presently, he disappeared. His father came to me, saying, "I am troubled about Harry. He took a Bible and went off into the mountains almost three weeks ago, and they tell me he has gone up to such a mountain, a long piece off. I am afraid he is going insane."

I said, "Brother, do not worry yourself. One of these days, he will come down in the glory and power of God." I knew what was in that fellow's heart.

One day, he returned under such an anointing of the Spirit as I had never before witnessed on any life. Here was a soul who had never read the words of Jesus. He was a full-grown man, but he said to me, "I have never looked into the Bible, unless it was in my childhood. I knew nothing of it."

One day after that, he came to me, his face radiant, and said, "Brother Lake, did you know this was in the Bible?" and proceeded to read to me that familiar verse in the sixteenth chapter of Mark: *"These signs shall follow them that believe...they shall cast out devils"* (Mark 16:17). Looking up into my face with great earnestness, he said, "My! I wish I knew somebody who had a devil." I believe God had planned that situation, for I was reminded that in my mail a couple of days before had come a request for an insane son. The mother said, "As far as I can tell, my son has a devil," and her request was that we might come and pray that the devil might be cast out. So, I got the letter and handed it to him. He said, "Why, this is only two or three blocks from where I live." He said, "I am going to find that fellow, and then I am coming back for you."

And all the time I said, "Here is a newborn soul, just born unto God, whose vision enters into the real realm of God-power." I realized that my own spirit had not touched the degree of faith that was in his soul, and I thought, *I do not want to do a thing, or say one word, that will discourage that soul in the least.*

Presently, he came back and said, "Brother Lake, come on." We went and found a young man who had been mad from his birth. He was like a wild animal. He would not wear clothes and would smash himself or anybody else with anything that was given to him. He couldn't even have a dish to eat on. But in the center of the enclosure where he was, they had a large stone hollowed out, and they would put his food on that and let him eat it just like an animal.

We tried to catch him, but he was as wild as a lion. He would jump right over my head. Finally, his father said, "You will never catch him out here." This time, I realized what the situation meant. I had been somewhat of an athlete in my youth, and I said to Von Shield, "You get on one side, and if he comes to your side, you will take care of him, and if he comes to my side, I will take care of him."

Now, beloved, this all sounds strange, I know, but I'll never forget that afternoon as long as I live. As I looked across to the young man, Von Shield, I could see the lightning flash of faith, and I knew that if he got his hands on the insane child, the devil would come out.

Presently, he landed on my side of the bed, and in an instant Von Shield sprang over the bed, laid his hands on his head, and commanded that devil to come out. In two minutes, that lad was absolutely transformed and was a sane young man. The first moment of sanity he ever knew.

Sometime later, the family moved to another section of the country, so I have lost track of him.

One more incident in the man's life will help you to realize this thing. Among the Boer people, especially in the Transvaal, they were a pioneer people. They had moved from Cape Colony and lived among the natives there many years. Finally, they succeeded in establishing their own community and later a republic. They did not have the advantages of good schools. In fact, about the time they passed into the hands of the English, education was becoming a real factor. About the only educated person in a community was the Dutch Predicant. He is a real old aristocrat. The firstborn of houses is the Predicant, and everything else likewise. He is the lord of all he surveys and some more. I believe they were people with all authority that the priests of Ireland exercise over the people there.

I wanted to leave you with the conception of a Dutch predicant,[1] and then you can understand how a young fellow, unrecognized as a preacher, is situated when he begins to preach the gospel of Christ in a different manner than the predicant.

One day, when Von Shield was conducting a service with a couple of hundred people present, the predicant was there. He arose when he was teaching and told the people that they were being misled, etc., and that these things Von Shield was talking about were only calculated for the days of the apostles.

The young man, naturally, if he had been an ordinary young man, would have been somewhat nonplussed. But presently he said, "I will tell you how we will settle this thing. There is Miss LeRoux, whom we all know. She is stone blind in one eye and has been so for four years. You come here, and I will lay my hands on you and ask the Lord Jesus to make you well." And, picking up his Dutch Bible, he said, "And when He does, you will read that chapter," designating the chapter she was to read.

God Almighty met the fellow's faith. The woman's eye opened right then, and she stood before that congregation and, covering the good eye, read with the eye that had been blind, the entire chapter. I know her well; I had visited at their home a great many times.

Now I will return to the other young man, the most extraordinary incident that I have known in the life of any other human being, unless it was the history of St. Paul when he was on his way to Damascus, when suddenly there shone around about him a light, brighter than the sun, and he says, "When we were all fallen to the earth." They were probably on horseback.

I heard a voice speaking unto me, and saying in the Hebrew tongue, Saul, Saul, why persecutest thou me? it is hard for thee to kick against the pricks. And I said, Who art thou, Lord? And he said, I am Jesus whom thou persecutes. (Acts 26:14–15)

---

1. *predicant*: a minister in the Dutch Reformed Church, especially in South Africa.

Kratzmall was visiting one night at the home of some friends, a few doors from my home. These young people with whom he was visiting had just recently been baptized in the Spirit themselves, and they were very anxious about this friend and had been praying a great deal about it. This same night he was in the tabernacle, and his friends said, "Come down to our home." So he went.

These two men, Kratzmall and Von Shield, were the highest developed men. I believe Kratzmall was physically the strongest man I ever met. He was an altogether unusual character. And here was a dealing of the Spirit of God such as I have never known with any other individual.

After a time, I believe it was suggested that they pray. He was going to stay all night. Harry said in speaking of it afterward, "It was not my custom to kneel. As I sat in my chair, I began to realize that a peculiar power was taking hold of me. I said, 'This must be some sort of a psychological condition that I am not familiar with. Anyway, I will have nothing to do with it.'" And he sat up in his chair and shut his teeth and endeavored to resist. The Spirit of God intensified, and he said, "I will not yield."

For two-and-a-half hours, he sat there while the perspiration poured off his person, until there were little pools of perspiration oozing from his shoes. But, at the end, as this battle was going on, a voice spoke within him and said, "I am Jesus."

And instantly he said, "If You are the Christ, You can do anything You like." The next moment, the Spirit of God deepened upon him, and he began to speak in tongues by the power of God.

Kratzmall, after that anointing, became the most remarkable preacher of the gospel I have ever known anything about. He traveled that country from end to end when he didn't have a cent. I met him once when he had no shoes and his feet were cut and bleeding. But he established congregations of Christian people for three hundred and fifty miles out through the wilderness. Bless God.

Now then, I will return. I have told you these incidents in order to demonstrate to you that there is a force in the Christian life that mankind has not gotten hold of in any great degree. But the thing that interests me most, and I endeavor to present to you the facts of a Christian life, is the inquiry that comes to me day by day from souls whom I deal with in the healing room: "How can I enter into the consciousness of the presence and power of Christ?"

> "How can I enter into the consciousness of
> the presence and power of Christ?"
> is the real issue in all our hearts.

That is the real issue in all our hearts. We see the thing that was burning in the heart of Nicodemus when he came to Jesus in the nighttime and said,

Rabbi, we know that thou art a teacher come from God: for no man can do these miracles that thou doest, except God be with him.
(John 3:2)

But Jesus, disregarding all that, said,

Except a man be born again, he cannot see the kingdom of God.... That which is born of the flesh is flesh; and that which is born of the Spirit is spirit. Marvel not that I said unto thee, Ye must be born again.
(John 3:3, 6–7)

The birth again of God, the conscious incoming of the Spirit of God into the life and being and personality, lifts mankind out of the condition of the professing Christian experience into the place of divine consciousness and power.

The baptism of the Holy Spirit was the common experience of New Testament times. The New Testament was written by men who had the baptism of the Holy Spirit. It was written to churches that possessed the baptism of the Holy Ghost. Indeed, in my study of the New Testament, the disciples seemed to consider it essential that each individual should himself possess the baptism of the Spirit. When Paul came down to Ephesus, the first question he asked them was,

> *Have ye received the Holy Ghost since ye believed? And they said unto him, We have not so much as heard whether there be any Holy Ghost. And he said unto them, Unto what then were ye baptized? And they said, Unto John's baptism.* (Acts 19:2–3)

And then he explained what John's baptism was. He said,

> *John verily baptized with the baptism of repentance, saying unto the people, that they should believe on him which should come after him, that is, on Christ Jesus.* (verse 4)

Then he laid his hands upon them, and they received the Holy Ghost and began to speak with tongues and magnify God and prophesy, etc.

There are only five cases on record in the New Testament of persons receiving the baptism of the Spirit:

1. The church at Jerusalem

2. The one hundred twenty, in the second chapter of Acts

3. The church at Samaria under the ministry of Peter and John. That is the case of Simon, the Sorcerer. When he witnessed the manifestation of power that occurred at the hands of the apostles, he offered them money, saying, "*Give me also this power, that on whomsoever I lay hands, he may receive the Holy Ghost*" (Acts 8:19). But you remember the answer: "*Thy money perish with thee, because thou hast thought that the gift of God may be purchased with money*" (Acts 8:20).

4. The next case is in the tenth chapter of Acts, where the Gentile church was baptized in the Holy Spirit.

5. Finally, in the household of Cornelius, as Peter preached the Word. No altar services there. No laying on of hands. There the Holy Ghost fell on all those who believed.

And, to this hour, it is my conviction that the real manner in which the Lord desires to pour out the Spirit in these days is the Spirit simply falling on listening believers. We had mighty few altar services or prayer services, but the power fell upon the people as they sat hearing the Word of God. I have witnessed the Lord baptize fifty people in an ordinary service like this on a Sunday evening.

There is a consciousness that seems to me by the Word of God and by my own personal experience to be possessed where any individual can enter into the direct presence of God and receive the baptism of the Spirit. That is the consciousness of *sinlessness*—the consciousness that your sins are gone. You can classify sin in any way you like. There is this much about it, that in our own inner soul we know that sin is offensive to God, because it is offensive to our own spirit.

So, as I said before, the consciousness of sinlessness seems to be God's requirement for those who would seek the baptism of the Spirit. Indeed, I remember in my own experience when my heart began to be stirred along this line, and I definitely began to seek God for the baptism of the Spirit, that, as the illumination of the purity and holiness of God began to dawn over my soul, instead of going on boldly, there was an inclination to draw back as I realized the awful extreme between my own heart and the heart of God. And I was compelled to cry out, not once but a thousand times, "Lord God, by the divine process of God, cleanse my soul from this condition." And I remember, bless God, how that one night I was present in a friend's home. An ordinary meeting was going on, conducted by a little Quaker woman, but she outlined what seemed to me to be the method of cleansing the soul.

That night, as I knelt in Fred Bosworth's home, that consciousness of the cleansing power of Jesus Christ went through my being, and I realized something of what I never realized before: that the battle between my spirit and my soul had ceased and that God reigned, not only in my spirit, but in my flesh, too. The war that had been in my spirit for years was all gone, and I entered into Beulah land. I really felt that I had crossed the Jordan and everything was new.

> The external evidences of God and the power of His Spirit are a small matter compared with the consciousness of the Word of God in the human heart.

I tell you, beloved, that the external evidences of God and the power of His Spirit, no matter how wonderful, are a small matter compared with the consciousness of the Word of God in the human heart; in your heart and mine, bless God.

In the fourteenth chapter of John, there is this one verse. While Jesus was discussing this subject with the disciples, He said, "He is with you"—that is, the Comforter. "He is with you, and *shall be in you.*" (See John 14:17.)

There is a definite possession of the Spirit of God by which the individual becomes the conscious possessor of the Spirit of God. Indeed, the Word of God puts it in this forceful manner: *"Know ye not that your body is the temple of the Holy Ghost which is in you?"* (1 Corinthians 6:19). It is God's purpose, as outlined by Jesus Christ and this Word from cover to cover, that man shall be the conscious possessor of the Spirit of the living God, the Holy Ghost.

That is the "real Christian." That is the thing that has been lacking in the church throughout the centuries past. It was that consciousness of God's presence and God's power in the disciples and the church of the first centuries that wrote across the pages of history the wonderful, wonderful record of Christianity of the first four hundred years. There were thirty million Christian martyrs, those who were slaughtered in the Christian wars, etc. Thirty million gave up their lives for the Christ. There was a spirit that made it so intense, so powerful, that had such a power of induction, that the world had to get out. Bless God.

But there came a day when the church traded the communion of the Holy Ghost for the smile of the world, and then the long, long night of the middle centuries followed.

But, bless God, I tell you we are living in a day and hour when the Spirit of God has come into the world afresh, when the consciousness of mankind is opening up to God in a manner that it has never opened before. There is an awakening in the world from ocean to ocean, from pole to pole, as there never was before. And I believe, bless God, that God Almighty's outpouring of the Spirit upon all flesh is at hand. And though we are receiving the droppings and our hearts are being warmed under the impulse of the Spirit, the day is not far distant when the flame of God will catch the soul of mankind. And the church of the latter day will close this era with a place of divine glory excelling that of the early church.

This is according to the prophecy of the Word: "If the former rain was abundant, shall not the latter rain be more abundant?" (See Deuteronomy 11:14.) Bless God.

If the disciples, without the train of Christian history behind them that you and I have, were able to enter into the divine consciousness and power of the Holy Spirit in such a way that they left a stamp upon Christianity, how much more shall men and women who have the advantage of two thousand years of Christian record enter into a diviner consciousness than ever the apostles possessed?

Interpretation of a Message in Tongues

The eternal God hath ordained that mankind, being united with Him as one heart and as one soul, shall glorify the Lord Jesus Christ in manifesting His life and character, His person and being.

Interpretation of a Second Message in Tongues

If, then, God's purpose for mankind is to receive the Christ, shall we not yield ourselves body and soul and spirit to the conscious control of the Spirit of God and let Him manifest Himself in us in humbleness and meekness, bowing lowly at the feet of Him whose we are and whom we serve?

> Down in the human heart,
> Crushed by the tempter,
> Feelings lie buried that grace can restore.
>
> Touched by a loving heart,
> Wakened by kindness,
> Chords that were broke will vibrate once more.

Prayer

Our God, we ask Thee tonight that Thy almighty power shall be upon each soul. That, as we endeavor to yield ourselves to Thee for the conscious cleansing of our nature from sin and its effects, Thy power shall lift us into that consciousness of oneness with God whereby from Thy soul to our own will flow the divine unction of God. That we, being cleansed from sin, may manifest God to mankind, so that the hungry world and dying race and wandering world may be brought back into oneness with God. Amen.

2

HOW TO RECEIVE ETERNAL LIFE: SOME FACTS ABOUT ETERNAL LIFE

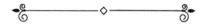

Eugene, Oregon

There are three Greek words that are translated "life" in the New Testament. The first word is *psuche*, which is the life of a fallen man; it is used to describe life of the animal world. God discriminates. The second word is *bios*, which is the manner of living or existence. Then comes the all-important word *zoe*, which is eternal life. This last word is used one hundred thirty times in the New Testament. Here is the remarkable thing about it: the word *psuche* and the word *zoe* are never used interchangeably. (See and compare STRONG G5590, G979, and G2222.)

The Holy Spirit uses *zoe* always in connection with eternal life, the divine life, the life that comes into the spirit of the believer. *Psuche* is never used in that sense. *Bios* is never used in that sense.

If thinking men could just discover what I am giving to you, if our scholars and our great teachers would carefully analyze the thing I am giving you, it would shake the foundation of biology absolutely.

Do you know, brethren, there isn't any chance for a man to be a skeptic if he knows anything about the Bible? Skepticism is simply ignorance gone to seed. But let me say it again: A man is skeptical about a thing that he doesn't know. You are not skeptical about a thing that you do know.

"Oh," a fellow says, "you cannot know anything about that." Well, that is not me. I can and do. I have been studying this marvelous Book for more than forty years. For twenty-seven or twenty-eight years, I have been using analytical studies or scientific methods in the study of the Scriptures; and I have arrived at the place where I absolutely know that this Book is not a human production. No human being could produce it.

I want to tell you, people, that the man who believes this Book and gives a little time to analytical studies, knows that he believes something that no human mind could produce. It is a supernatural book. Someone says, "No man believes in the supernatural now." I want to say that all the sensible people do believe in the supernatural. It is those little, narrow-minded folks that knock miracles. Big men, real men, men who are thinking through, men whose thumb or finger is upon the pulse of universal consciousness, absolutely know that miracles are demanded by universal man.

Do you know that these fellows who have only half thought through, who have walked around the truth and never gone through it, don't know what they are talking about? If you want to master a thing, think through it. I know it will make your brains sweat, but brain sweat is the sign of genius. Real men sweat in their brains.

Now, eternal life is the biggest problem of the human experience. If I wanted to give a great oratorical address, there isn't any subject that would intrigue me and challenge me like this. Let me show you what I mean.

Over in Job, the oldest book of the Bible, the great, outstanding question is how to get this thing called eternal life. The problem of Plato was the craving for eternal life. Every one of the old religions came into being because man craved eternal life. Cannibalism came out of the passion in man for eternal life. He laid his offering on the altar, and he said, "If I can drink the blood and eat some of the flesh, I will eat God, and then I will become immortal and live eternally."

The only man who wants to die like a beast is the man who is living below the beast. Real men want to live. Real men rise in rebellion against the very thought that death means extinction.

Ladies and gentlemen, I have only begun thinking. I have only begun living. If I could have fifty years more, I could do something. But, I am going to have an eternity, and I am going to associate with all the princes and the queens and all the great men and the great women of the ages, eternally.

A few years ago, people asked me to preach on heaven, and I said, "No, I guess not. It is more important that I preach on the present." And I went away, but the idea kept growing in me. I do not know why.

I have always been popular in preaching funeral sermons. Folks want me to come and say pretty things.

By and by one day, I said to myself, "I am going to study this heaven business." The result was this: I made a discovery that heaven was the center around which all the ministry of Jesus and the teaching of Jesus revolved. He told us, *"I came forth from the Father, and am come into the world: again I leave the world, and go to the Father"* (John 16:28), and *"In my Father's house are many mansions:…I go to prepare a place for you"* (John 14:2).

I found out that the book of Revelation has a new heaven and new earth. I found out that God majored on the subject of heaven. The reason is this: we are eternal beings. You may fiddle around about it all you have a mind to, but you are eternal. You may have philosophical and metaphysical religions; yet, when it comes down to the real heart of things, you will want a religion that is not man-made, and you will want a religion that gives a safe bridge across from time into eternity and makes heaven an absolute surety.

When it comes down to the real heart of things, you will want a religion that is not man-made, a religion that gives a safe bridge across from time into eternity and makes heaven an absolute surety.

I said that the only man who wants to die like a brute is the man who has lived lower than a brute. Do you know, men and women, that Christianity is the only religion among all the religions of the world that gives a clear conception, a clear teaching, about heaven? Why? All the old religions of the world are human religions. What do I mean by that? They are religions that have been born in the mind of a man. Christianity is born in the heart of God the Father.

The eternal life fact is the greatest fact of human experience. Universal man has craved it. Drinking the blood and eating offerings came because the heart craved and reached out for it. It is the parent of all religions. Kings took the names of their gods because they wanted union with God. Man has wanted union with deity through all the ages.

Theosophy,[2] which claims to be the consummation of all religions, has as its basic thesis this statement: all men have God in them; all men have union with God. That is the basic thesis of Theosophy. That is not true, but Theosophy has gathered all the cry of universal man and attempted with human philosophy to answer that cry.

Jesus came and answered the cry, and Jesus hasn't given us any philosophy. Did you ever think of it? Jesus hasn't given us any metaphysics. Jesus has given us the thing we wanted, and He has given it so we know it. You can outgrow—and you will outgrow—any philosophy, any system of metaphysics, any human religion, but you can't outgrow God's life imparted to you. Do you see it? You cannot outgrow real Christianity. It can't be outgrown.

---

2. *Theosophy*: the teachings of a modern movement originating in the United States in 1875 and following chiefly Buddhist and Brahmanic theories especially of pantheistic evolution and reincarnation.

A man said, "Say, Doctor, do you know that So-and-so, who is a Christian, has turned over his church and joined a cult?"

I said, "He is not a Christian man." Friends, I challenge you that no Christian ever received Jesus Christ and then went into a philosophical religion. I have never known it. If you could bring me one case—but you can't—that is all. It is an impossibility unless the man's mind had broken. Why? Well, I will tell you why. The moment I was born again and the great, mighty Holy Spirit came into my life, do you know I reached the ultimate right there? And there has been nothing that challenged me for one minute. I have read everything. I have listened to every man who had anything to offer. I never heard anything but words—beautiful words, yes, but they are just words of man. I have found God.

Let me illustrate. Years ago, I was giving a series of addresses in Boston. It was when the American Teacher's Association met in Boston. I was advertising for my meeting. Down at the door, I had this big word printed: "Reality." I was watching the people as they came in. A fine-looking man stood looking, and then he said, "That is a good word. Do you know I have been a truth seeker for years?"

I said, "You will pardon me, but I have found it."

Just so long as you are seeking, you haven't found. You have found a great deal, but you have not found the *"pearl of great price"* (Matthew 13:46). Let me say to you, men and women, that as long as you are a seeker, you are not a finder. You may be seeking more of the thing that you have, but you are perfectly content with the kind and the quality and the thing that you have. You have found God. You may long to know your Father better, but that is altogether different than being a truth seeker.

And to that man, I replied, "I have found it."

He said, "What do you mean?"

I said, "I beg your pardon, but I am the man who is going to speak."

He said, "Do you know that I have been through the whole thing?"

I said, "Through what?"

"Through this church business."

I said, "This is not church business. This is reality. I know what you are talking about, but you are talking about something you don't know anything about. This thing I am talking about is real, and when you have found it, you stop searching. You have arrived. To use an Americanism, you have 'got it!'"

Men and women, do you understand that when you have received eternal life, you have arrived? Let me illustrate. The disciples had been across the Sea of Galilee. They had fed five thousand that afternoon. They had had a marvelous time. They had seen miracles of God that had staggered them. Jesus had gone up into the mountain to pray and told them to get in the boat and go across. They rowed and rowed. The wind was against them, and they could not make any headway. In the midst of the storm, they saw Jesus walking on the waves. It frightened them. But Jesus drew near and He spoke, and they answered Him, and they knew it was Him. Here is what happened. Jesus walked up beside the boat and stepped into it and no sooner than He did, that boat scraped its hull on the shore of Capernaum. What does Capernaum mean? It means contentment. The moment that Jesus was in the boat, they arrived. That is all. (See John 6:5–21.)

And I say to you tonight that the moment Jesus steps over the gunwales of your boat and into your life, you are there. Now, Christianity is life, not a religion. It is a real life and relationship. It is a union of God and man—not the masses, but the individual. He imparts to us His very nature, His very life.

Christianity is life, not a religion. It is a real life and relationship. It is a union of God and man.

I am going to talk to you from another angle. Before we can fully grasp this, it is necessary to go over a little old ground. You see, man was created because God longed for children. God created the world as the habitation of His man, and then He created man in His own image, after His own likeness. (See Genesis 1:26–27.) Now, the object of man's creation was that God might have children. He was child-hungry. You can understand that.

God's heart was the reason for man. What kind of a man would it be natural for Him to create if He created a man to be His child? He would create a man in His own class, in His own image, after His own likeness. That would be normal.

Now, God is a Spirit, so then, man must be a spirit. He has a soul, intellect, affections, and will, but he lives in a body. You say, "What is His conscience?" Consciousness is the voice of man's spirit. It is the spirit speaking. But you say, "Hasn't man a subconscious mind?" No, that is psychological nonsense. The thing we call the subconscious mind is simply your own spirit, the real man. Jesus illustrated it. You are cognizant that there is something above your intellect. There is somebody that makes you think when you don't want to. There is something above your reason that makes you think when you are tired. You can watch yourself, and, after a little while, the spirit will separate from your intellect and other faculties, so you will be cognizant of it.

Your spirit is the mother of faith and the mother of love and the mother of hatred. Joy lives in your spirit. Happiness is in your mind. Happiness depends upon circumstances; joy depends upon God. Nobody has any joy but the spirit who is in fellowship with God.

Let's go a little farther. Man was created a spirit being. Why? So that God could impart to him His nature. Your spirit is the part of you that receives the nature of God. Your mind can't know God. You cannot know God by study. If you could find God intellectually, you would find Him in the laboratory, but you can't find God that way. Scientists have done a lot of loose talking about it. However, God is not known by the intellect but by the spirit.

You know a lot of things that you cannot give a reason for. They are above your reasoning. Now, your spirit is the part of you that comes in touch with God. Your mind comes in touch with things intellectually. Your spirit is the part of you that comes in contact with God.

Another angle is this: You people who are deeply spiritual have had contacts with God that were beyond your reason, and you could not explain it. Now, what part of man is born again? His spirit. That is the part of you that is *"renewed after the image of Him that created him"* (Colossians 3:10). The new birth is because you have come out of Satan's family into God's family; that is the new birth. There is nothing mysterious about it. It is just as simple as any other fact of human experience.

I venture to say this: The new birth, receiving eternal life, can be classed among the certain sciences. It can be placed on scientific grounds. You do three things, and you will receive eternal life as sure as you sit in that chair. I don't care whether you are at the Arctic Circle or the equator.

Now, that is scientific. That is absolutely in the realm of science. Every scholar knows that. A thing is scientific when every single demonstration arrives at a single conclusion. Four plus four is eight. Nine plus nine is eighteen. That is scientific.

You do three things, and you are born again as sure as God sits on the throne. That is scientific. I want to tell you that prayer is based on scientific grounds. I have found it out.

In John 10:10, Jesus said: *"I am come that they might have life, and that they might have it more abundantly."*

That means have it in profusion; have it without stint or limitation. That staggers you. That is big. That brings us out into the open with it. *"I am come that [you] might have life"*—His life, God's life, God's nature.

The Bible tells us in Ephesians 2:3 that we *"were by nature the children of wrath."* It tells us in 2 Peter 1:4 that we become *"partakers of the divine nature,*" which is the biggest thing in the world. What is eternal life? It is the nature of God. Jesus brought that to me.

Why didn't God give it before Jesus came? Because God had no legal right to give it. In the first place, man was spiritually dead. He had committed high treason against God. It was necessary that God be vindicated and that man be redeemed. Eternal life, then, is the nature of God, and God gave it to man on legal grounds.

> *That as sin hath reigned* [as king] *unto death, even so might grace reign through righteousness unto eternal life by Jesus Christ our Lord.*   (Romans 5:21)

It means that grace is based on righteousness. When God wanted to give eternal life to man, He did it on legal grounds. Had God given eternal life on any other basis, it would not be God doing it, because God is just and righteous.

If God had said, "Now, I pity the human race; I am sorry for them. I am going to give them eternal life," you could not trust Him any more than you can the devil. But when Jesus died, He paid the penalty of man's transgression. Then God could legitimately and justly give eternal life to man.

God had a right to give eternal life because He purchased it with His Son's blood. The supreme court of the universe has endorsed Jesus's death and substitutionary sacrifice and accepted it. Then, God had a right to give eternal life to us. It is the greatest blessing that ever came to man.

We know we have passed from death unto life. What is God's nature? It is love. Then, what is the normal thing for me to do? It is to live. The moment He gives it to me, I become a "liver." "*We know that we have passed from death unto life, because we love the brethren*" (1 John 3:14).

Hear this, beloved:

Every one that loveth is born of God, and knoweth God. He that loveth not knoweth not God.   (1 John 4:7–8)

Everyone who does not love is not born again. There is the touchstone. The moment that you are born again is the moment that the nature and life of God come into your spirit.

What action [effect] does that have on your intellect? That is the greatest fact of the biological study. You take a young fellow sixteen or seventeen years of age, and he has a chum about the same years. They are in the same class in school. They have made the same grades from kindergarten up, and as far as you can see, they are just the same. Now, one of them receives eternal life—he is born again—and he has proper instructions at home and in his church. In three months' time, the boy who has received eternal life will be ten percent more effective than his chum. He is from ten to twenty percent more efficient than the boy who has not been born again, and he will hold that ratio if he walks with God.

Why shouldn't it be? Three things happen. First, he has received God's nature, and that is reacting on his intellect. That ought to help him some. Second, he has no condemnation. That is gone. And the third thing, he has somebody to rest him all the time. He depends on the strength of another. The other boy can't do it.

Now, I want to carry you a step beyond this. You know, men and women, that the children who are born to a Christian man and a Christian woman are mentally of a higher order, and they are a finer texture morally than those born of the unsaved. I have proved that beyond a shadow of a doubt.

Another startling thing is this: Take a man and a woman who are not Christians. They have two or three children. Then they are born again, and they have three more children. The last three are mentally superior to the first three. They are more easily managed, and they are more beautiful.

Gentlemen, if this was taught in our colleges, ninety percent of our young men and women in our colleges would become Christians. Every intelligent young woman wants to raise the highest quality of children possible, as well as do the high-minded type of young men. What man looks forward to raising children who are mentally below what they should be? Every real man wants to give his child the very finest and the best.

I have statistics to prove that out of the four hundred great businesses in the United States, like the sugar and lumber trusts, thirty percent of the men who are managing the greatest industries are sons of clergymen. Out of four hundred, one hundred twenty are the sons of clergymen who are directing the great business enterprises. Twenty-five percent are the sons of bankers and lawyers, etc., but the sons of clergymen make up thirty percent.

Clergymen's children have the hardest opportunity of any, because the average minister doesn't stay but about seventeen months in one place until he moves. His children are pulled out of school continually, and yet they outstrip all the other boys combined. Why? Because the average old-fashioned preacher was born again, and his children grew up in a godly home.

Did you know, men and women, that men like William Jennings Bryant, Beveridge,[3] and others that have given the best things we have had for sixty years, are the sons of Christian men? Did you know that the editors, like the editor of the *Saturday Evening Post*, the *Ladies Home Journal,* and the other great papers of this country, are all ministers' sons? They are not all Christians, but their fathers and mothers had eternal life and that eternal life reacted in these children.

> Christianity is the life of God coming into a man. This is the biggest thing you ever faced in your life.

---

3. Albert Jeremiah Beveridge, 1862–1927, American politician and historian (MWD).

I want to tell you that Christianity is not a religion. Christianity is the life of God coming into a man. This is the biggest thing you ever faced in your life, gentlemen. I could pour statistics on you that would carry you off your feet. I know, gentlemen, that Christianity is the life of God in a man. And the greatest crime that is ever committed against our children is to take Jesus away from them. A father who will not give his children Jesus is a criminal in the sight of God and thinking men and women. Listen, men. Out on our prairies, we raise hogs and cattle and sheep for the eastern market. In our homes, we raise children for the devil.

A good farmer would not allow a diseased animal in his herd or his flock, but you allow any kind of woman to come into your house and fellowship with your children, or any kind of man. He may be as rotten as hell. He may damn your boy, and then you say, "I don't think it is a fair deal that God would damn my boy." You never gave God a square deal. The biggest thing in all the world is man's union with Deity.

I am not preaching religion. I have come down to brass tacks in this thing. This is the biggest thing you ever faced in your life.

Here is the thing, gentlemen. It is your receiving into your spirit the nature and life of God. "But," you ask, "how can I do it?" Here is the genius of God. God did not say, "If you are 6'4" or 5'7", you can have eternal life," or, "If you can pass the high school grades, you can have it," or, "If you are worth one million dollars, you can have it." But He said, "If you believe, you can have it."

There are two things that are as natural as breathing: faith and unbelief. Unbelief comes from ignorance, and faith comes from the Word of God. Faith is the normal thing in life. Everything in life is based on faith.

You came here tonight believing that you would get back home. You buy a suit of clothes believing that they will meet your need. You marry on faith. You put your money in the bank on faith. Everything about your life is based on faith. Every human relationship is a faith relationship. You have been acting on faith all your life. You say you haven't the faculty? You mean you have got a disobedient complex.

What is faith? That you dig into this Book and you come to God and you say, "God, as far as I know, that Book is true." You say, "As many as receive Him, to them gave He the right to become the children of God." (See John 1:12.) You pray, "Now, I want to be Your child. I will take Jesus Christ as my Savior." Then you say, "I must confess Him as my Lord" because it says:

> *If thou shalt confess with thy mouth the Lord Jesus, and shalt believe in thine heart that God hath raised him from the dead, thou shalt be saved.* (Romans 10:9)

What does God ask? Just this: "If you will take My Son as Savior and confess to the world His Lordship, I will give you eternal life." Isn't that the simplest thing you ever heard in your life?

"If you will take My Son to be your Savior and confess Him before the world as your Lord, I will give you eternal life." That is the easiest thing in the world.

Three things:

+ Do you believe that Jesus died and rose for you? Yes.

+ Next, do you take Him as your Savior? Yes.

+ Will you confess Him to the world? Yes.

And as sure as you do it, I will stake my life and everything I have in this world that God will not break His Word. If you will take Jesus Christ as your Savior, and confess Him as Lord, God will give you eternal life.

Someone says, "I don't know whether I have it or not." If you have it, you absolutely know you have. Don't pretend you have it when you don't know. But if you haven't it, you can have it where you are tonight, and you say, "The first chance I get, I will confess Him as Lord." If you do, God will give you eternal life. You can go to the altar if you like, but there is only one thing you have to do, take Him as your Savior and confess Him as your Lord, and God will take you to be His child. I have seen thousands upon thousands settle the issue.

3

TRIUNE SALVATION

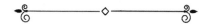

Sermon also delivered in Washington, D.C.

This sermon was delivered in London, England, by Reverend John G. Lake at a conference of the Church of England ministry presided over by Ingram, Bishop of London, who said,

> It contains the spirit of primitive Christianity and reveals the distinction between the Christian soul of the first and twentieth century, the Spirit of Christ dominion, by which primitive Christianity attained its spiritual supremacy.... It is one of the greatest sermons I have ever heard, and I recommend its careful study by every priest.
>
> Mr. Lake had been invited to address us and has traveled 7,000 miles to be here. A committee of the Church of England was sent to South Africa to investigate Mr. Lake, his work, his power, his teaching, and his ministry. His presence here is the result of their satisfactory report.

Scripture Test

I pray God your whole spirit and soul and body be preserved blameless [without defilement, corruption] unto the coming of our Lord Jesus Christ. Faithful is he that calleth you, who also will do it.
(1 Thessalonians 5:23–24)

In the beginning of all things, even before the creation of man at all, there was a condition in which all things that then existed were obedient to God. Angels were obedient to the Lord. But there came a time when angels themselves rebelled against the government of God. In Isaiah, Satan is spoken of as *"Lucifer, son of the morning"* (Isaiah 14:12). Again, the Word says in substance concerning him, "Wast thou not pure and holy until pride was found in thine heart?" (See Isaiah 14:13–14.)

Pride was the condition which, in the angel who was pure and holy, generated the desire to be separated from God and to rebel against Him.

It was the same pride, or desire to substitute his will for the will of God, which caused Adam to sin. From Adam, humanity has derived the same instinctive desire to insist on their way instead of God's way. Through the continued exercise of the human will and the world's way, the race has drifted into misty conceptions of the real will and the real way of God. This is particularly true in regard to the nature and substance of God.

It seems difficult to think of Him as a Being and a Substance. God is Spirit, but Spirit is a materiality. And God Himself is a materiality—a heavenly, not an earthly, materiality. The forms of angels are a substance; otherwise, they would not be discernible. It is not an earthly substance or material but a heavenly one.

As we think of the substance of which heavenly beings are composed and of which God Himself must necessarily be a composition, the mind settles on light and fire and spirit as a possibility.

Then the Word tells us that God breathed into Adam the breath of life, and man became a living soul. (See Genesis 2:7.) There came a time when God made man. The Word tells us that He made man's body of the substance of the earth. (See Genesis 2:7.) He made man, the Word says, *"in his own image, in the image of God created he him"* (Genesis 1:27); not just in the form that God was, but God breathed into him His own self, His own being—that heavenly materiality of which God consists. He injected or breathed Himself into the man, and the man then became a composition of that heavenly substance, or materiality and earth, or the substance of the earth.

Adam was the created son of God. He was just like God. He was just as pure as God was pure. God fellowshipped with him. The Word of God tells us that God came down into the garden in the cool of the day and walked with Adam and talked with Adam. There was perfect fellowship between God and Adam. He was a sinless man. He could look right into the face of God, and his eyes and his spirit did not draw back. The purity of God did not startle him. He was just as pure as God was pure. That was the original man.

Man, being composed of God and of heaven—of a heavenly materiality—and his body of the earth, being a sovereign like God, made him equal with God in sinlessness. God treated him with equality and gave him dominion over the earth. Man was a reigning sovereign on the earth.

Everything—all conditions, spiritual and physical—were subject to that God-man. The way of sin was this: that man chose to follow the inclinations of his earth-being, his animal consciousness, or his body instead of his God-man, God-being, or spirit. The result was that because of the suggestion of Satan, there developed calls of the earth for the earthly. After a while, he partook of things earthly and became earthly himself. Therefore, the fall of man was his fall into himself. He fell into his own earthly self, out of his heavenly estate, and the separation was absolute and complete.

God had said, *"But of the tree of the knowledge of good and evil, thou shalt not eat of it: for in the day that thou eatest of thereof [sin], thou shalt surely die"* (Genesis 2:17). That is, "In the day you sin—partaking of that which is earthy, the conditions of the earth being that of decay—the death process begins." So death reigned from the time that sin came.

> The fall of man was his fall into himself. He fell into his own earthly self, out of his heavenly estate, and the separation was absolute and complete.

Sickness is incipient death. Death is the result of sin. There is no sickness in God. There never was, there never will be, and there never can be. There was no sickness in man—in the God-man—until such time as he became the earth-man; until, by the operation of will, he sank into himself and became of the earth, earthy. Therefore, sin is the parent of sickness in that broad sense. Sickness is the result of sin. There could have been no sickness if there had been no sin.

Man, having fallen into that condition and being separated from God, needed a Redeemer. Redemption was a necessity because the Word says, *"Ye must be born again"* (John 3:7). God had to provide a means of getting man back into the original condition in which he had once been. One man cannot save another because one man is of the earth—earthy, even as another is—and man in the natural cannot save another. One cannot elevate another into a spiritual condition or put that one in a spiritual condition that is not in himself.

Thus, it became necessary for God, in order to redeem the race, to provide a means of reuniting God and man. So Jesus was born, even as Adam had been made. He was begotten of God—He was born of God—but He partook of the tendencies of the natural life and received His natural, physical body through His mother, Mary. The Word of God speaks of the first Adam and the last Adam. (See 1 Corinthians 15:45.) They were both Adams. They both came to produce a race. The first Adam had fallen and sinned. Therefore, the race that was produced through him was a race of sinful people with the same tendencies in their natures that were in his.

The last Adam, Jesus, had no sin. He had exactly the same privileges that the first Adam had. He could have sinned if He so chose. Jesus was a man in this world, just as every man is. *"He took not on him the nature of angels; but he took on him the seed of Abraham"* (Hebrews 2:16.) He did not take upon Himself a heavenly condition. He took upon Himself the natural condition of the human family—fallen human nature.

> It became necessary for God, in order to redeem the race, to provide a means of reuniting God and man.

But Jesus Christ triumphed over that condition of fallen human nature and did not sin, though the Word of God emphasizes that He *"was in all points tempted like as we are, yet without sin"* (Hebrews 4:15). The Word also says that Jesus is able to save or deliver (*"succour"* KJV) those who are tempted, having Himself been tempted even as we are tempted. (See Hebrews 2:18.) This is what makes Him a sympathetic Savior and Christ.

The purpose of Jesus in the world was to show us the Father. So, Jesus came and committed Himself publicly at His baptism at the Jordan before all the world *"to fulfil all righteousness"* (Matthew 3:15)— to do the will of God. He willed not to obey His own natural human will, but to do the will of the Father and to be wholly and solely and entirely obedient to the will of God. He declared, *"I came...not to do mine own will, but the will of him that sent me"* (John 6:38).

When a Christian is born of God and becomes a real Christian, he is made a Christ-man. If the world wants to see Jesus, it must look upon the Christian who is the Christ-man, just as we who want to look upon the Father and understand Him look upon the man Jesus, who was the embodiment of the Father. Everything that Jesus did was the will and the Word of the Father. So, too, everything the Christian does, if he is a real one, should be the will and Word of Jesus Christ. The Christian commits himself as entirely to the will of Jesus and becomes a Christ-man as Jesus committed Himself to the will of the Father and became a God-man.

A low standard of Christianity is responsible for all the shame and sin and wickedness in the world. Many Christians think it is all right if they pattern after Jesus in a "sort of" way. They imitate Him, and they do the things that He did; that is, they outwardly do them. They perform kind acts, and they do other things which Jesus did. But the secret of Christianity is not in doing; the secret is in being. Real Christianity is in being a possessor of the nature of Jesus Christ. In other words, it is being Christ in character, Christ in demonstration, Christ in agency of transmission. When one gives himself to the Lord and becomes a child of God—a Christian—he is a Christ-man. All that he does and all that he says from that time on should be the will and the words and the doings of Jesus, just as absolutely, just as entirely, as He spoke and did the will of the Father.

> Real Christianity is being Christ in character, Christ in demonstration, Christ in agency of transmission.

Jesus gave us the secret of how to live this kind of life. He showed us that the only way to live this life is to commit oneself, as He did, to the will of God and not to walk in his own ways at all but to walk in God's ways. So, the one who is going to be a Christ-man in the best sense, and let the world see Jesus in him, must walk in all the ways of Jesus and follow Him. He must be a Christ-man—a Christian, or Christ-one.

Therefore, the things which possess the heart and which are unlike God fasten themselves because the inner being is not subject to the will of God. One of the reasons for this low standard of Christian living is the failure to recognize the trinity of our own being. Man is triune—body and soul and spirit—just the same as God is triune, being Father and Son and Holy Ghost.

Salvation begins at the time when the spirit is surrendered to God, when the name is written in the Book of Life, and when we receive the conscious knowledge of sins being forgiven. Then, God witnesses to the spirit that our sins are blotted out. The Word, in the eighth chapter of Romans, says, *"His Spirit itself beareth witness with our spirit, that we are the children of God"* (Romans 8:16). That is, the testimony of the Spirit of God to our spirit is that we are the children of God when we surrender our spirits to God.

People wonder why, after having given their hearts to God and after having received a witness of the Spirit, they are troubled with evil desires and tempted in evil ways. The nature has three departments; therefore, the surrender of the spirit to God is not all that He demands. God demands also the mind and the body.

The mind is the soul life, and it continues being of the earth—earthy—and doing earthy things until God does something; until we seek God for a new mind. It is similar to the change which occurs in the spirit, and the mind that formerly thought evil and had wicked conceptions becomes as the mind of Christ.

The church at large recognizes the salvation of the spirit. But it has not recognized the salvation of the mind from the power of sin, and that is why many church people will say there is no such thing as sanctification.

There are Christian bodies that believe in the power of God to sanctify this mind, even as the spirit is saved. John Wesley, in defining sanctification, said that it is: "possessing the mind of Christ, and all the mind of Christ." An individual with all the mind of Christ cannot have a thought that is not a Christ-thought, no more than a spirit fully surrendered to God could have evil within it.

In later years, as the revelation by the Spirit of God has gone on, man has begun to see that there is a deeper degree of salvation than these two. He is a triune being. As he needed salvation for the mind and spirit, so he has a body which needs to be transformed by God. The whole question of physical healing, the redemption of the body, and the possible translation—the resurrection—are included there.

Christ is a Savior of the whole man—of spirit, of soul, of body. When Jesus at the Jordan committed Himself unto all righteousness to His Father, He committed His body just as He committed His mind and just as He committed His spirit. Christians have not been taught to commit their bodies to God, and therefore they feel justified in committing them to someone else, or to something else, rather than to God.

> Christ is a Savior of the whole man—
> of spirit, of soul, of body.

Therefore, it is clear that in a whole salvation it is just as offensive to God to commit the body to the control of man as it would be to commit the spirit to man for salvation. Salvation for the spirit can come only through Jesus, through the blood of Christ, through receiving His Spirit. Salvation from natural thoughts and ways and the operation of the natural mind can come only through the natural mind being transformed into the mind of Christ. Salvation for the body is found in the same manner, by committing the body now and forever to God.

No one would think of sending to any other power than God for a remedy for the spirit. There is no spirit that one could go to, unless it is the spirit of the world or the spirit of the devil; and one goes not to either of these for the healing of the spirit or mind.

The real Christian is a separated man. He is separated forever unto God in all the departments of his life, and so his body and his soul and his spirit are forever committed to God. Therefore, from the day that he commits himself to God, he can go to no other power for help or healing except to God. This is what gives such tremendous force to such

Scriptures as this: *"Cursed be the man that trusteth in man, and maketh flesh his arm, and whose heart departeth from the* Lord*"* (Jeremiah 17:5). Second Chronicles relates that in the thirty-ninth year of his reign, Asa, the king of Israel, became diseased in his feet, and in his disease he trusted not the Lord but the physicians, and he died. Asa had been trusting God for many years by taking his little, insignificant army and delivering the great armies into his hand. But when he became diseased in his feet, he trusted not the Lord but the physicians, and that was the offense of Asa against God. (See 2 Chronicles 16:12–13.)

The impression I wish to leave is this: that a hundredfold consecration to God takes the individual forever out of the hands of all but God. This absolute consecration to God, this triune salvation, is the real secret of the successful Christian life.

When one trusts any department of his being to man, he is weak in that respect, and that part of his being is not committed to God. When we trust our minds (souls) and our bodies to man, two parts are out of the hands of God, and there remains only our spirits in tune with heaven. It ought not to be so. The committing of the whole being to the will of God is the mind of God. Blessed be His name.

Such a commitment of the being to God puts one in the place where, just as God supplies health to the spirit and health to the soul, he trusts God to supply health to his body. Divine healing is the removal, by the power of God, of the disease that has come upon the body. But divine health is to live day by day and hour by hour in touch with God, so that the life of God flows into the body just as the life of God flows into the mind or flows into the spirit.

The Christian, the child of God, the Christ-man, who thus commits himself to God ought not to be a subject for healing. He is a subject of continuous, abiding health. And the secret of life in communion with God, the Spirit of God, is received into the being, into the soul, into the spirit.

The salvation of Jesus was a redemption of the whole man from all the power of sin, every whit—sin in the spirit, sin in the soul, sin in the body. If salvation or redemption is from the power of sin and every sin in our being, then the effect that sin produces in us must disappear and leave when the source is healed. Thus, instead of remaining sick, the Christian who commits his body to God becomes at once—through faith—the recipient of the life of God in his body.

> The salvation of Jesus was a redemption of the whole man from all the power of sin, every whit—sin in the spirit, sin in the soul, sin in the body.

Jesus gave us an example of how perfectly the Spirit of God radiates not only from the spirit or from the mind, but from the body also. The transfiguration was a demonstration of the Spirit of God from within the man radiating out through his person until the illumination radiated through his clothes, and his clothes became white and glistening, and his face shone as the light. It was the radiation of God through his flesh.

In a few instances, God permitted me to see Christians thus illuminated in a measure. I am acquainted with a brother in Chicago whose face is illuminated all the time; there is a radiation from it. His countenance is never seen in a condition of depression or as if the pores of his flesh are closed. There is an unmistakable something that marks him as one through whom the Spirit of God radiates.

God radiated through the purified personality of Jesus so that even His very clothes became white and glistening. Christians are Christ-men and stand in the stead of Jesus. The Word of God says to the Christian and to the church: "Ye are His body." (See Ephesians 1:22–23; 5:29–30.) The accumulated company of those who know Jesus, who really have the God-life within, are the body of Christ in the world, and through that body of Christ all the ministry of Jesus is operative.

The nine gifts of the Holy Spirit are the divine equipment of God by which the church, His body, is forever to continue to do the works of Jesus.

The nine gifts of the Holy Spirit are the divine equipment of God by which the church, His body, is forever to continue to do the works of Jesus: "To one is given the word of wisdom, to another the word of knowledge, to another faith, to another the gifts of healing, to another working of miracles, to another prophecy, to another the interpretation of tongues." (See 1 Corinthians 12:8–10.) All these gifts Jesus exercised during His earthly ministry. The people who exercise these gifts create another practical Christ—the church which is His body, Christ being the head.

When this truth is seen, Christianity will be on a new-old basis. The illumination of God, the consciousness of our position in the world, the consciousness of our responsibility as the representatives of Christ, places upon us as Christ-men and Christ-women the burden of Christ for a lost world. Of necessity, this lifts the heart and spirit into a new contact with God and the consciousness that, if a son of God, if a Christ-man to the world, then one must be worthy of his Christ. The only way to be worthy is to be in the will of Jesus.

Men have mystified the gospel; they have philosophized the gospel. The gospel of Jesus is as simple as can be. As God lived in the body and operated through the man Jesus, so the man on the throne, Jesus, operates through His body, the church, in the world. Even as Jesus Himself was the representative of God the Father, so also the church is the representative of Christ. As Jesus yielded Himself unto all righteousness, so the church should yield herself to do the will of Christ.

"These signs shall follow them that believe" (Mark 16:17)—not the preacher or the elder or the priest but the believer. The believer shall speak in new tongues; the believer shall lay hands on the sick and they shall recover. (See Mark 16:17–18.) The believer is the body of Christ in the world. The Word says, "There shall be saviors in Zion." (See Obadiah 1:21.) As Jesus took us and lifted us up to the Father, and as He takes the church and lifts her to the Father and gave Himself to sanctify and cleanse her (see Ephesians 5:25–26), so the Christian takes the world and lifts it up to the Christ, *"the Lamb of God, which taketh away the sin of the world"* (John 1:29).

The wonderful simplicity of the gospel of Jesus is itself a marvel. The wonder is that men have not understood always the whole process of salvation. How was it that men mystified it? Why is it that we have not lived a better life? Because our eyes were dim and we did not see and we did not realize that God left us here in this world to demonstrate Him, even as the Father left Jesus in the world to demonstrate the Father.

The man with Christ in him—with the Holy Ghost—is greater than any other power in the world. All other natural and evil powers are less than God; even Satan himself is a lesser power. Man with God in him is greater than Satan. That is the reason that God says to the believer, "You shall cast out devils." (See Mark 16:17.) *"Greater is he that is in you, than he that is in the world"* (1 John 4:4). The Christian, therefore, is a ruler; he is in the place of dominion, the place of authority, even as Jesus was.

Jesus, knowing that all power had been given unto Him, took a basin and a towel and washed His disciples' feet. His power did not exalt Him. It made Him the humblest of all men. So the more a Christian possesses, the more of a servant he will be. God is the great servant of the world—the One who continually gives to men the necessity of the hour. Through His guidance and direction of the laws of the world, He provides for all the needs of mankind. He is the Great Servant of the world, the greatest of all servants.

Yea, Jesus, knowing that all power had been committed to Him, and as God gave the power to Jesus, so Jesus commits through the Holy Ghost, by His own Spirit, all power to man.

I tell you, beloved, it is not necessary for people to be dominated by evil or by evil spirits. Instead of being dominated, Christians should exercise dominion and control other forces. Even Satan has no power over them, only as they permit him to have. Jesus taught us to close the mind, to close the heart, to close the being, against all that is evil; to live with an openness to God only, so that the sunlight of God shines in. The glorious radiance of God shines in, but everything that is dark is shut out.

Jesus said, *"Take heed therefore how ye hear"* (Luke 8:18), not what you hear. One cannot help what he hears, but he can take heed how he hears. When it is something offensive to the Spirit and the knowledge of God, shut the doors of the nature against it, and it will not touch you. The Christian lives as God in the world, dominating sin, evil, and sickness, bless God. I would to God that He would help us to so present Jesus in the true light that this church, and the church that is in the world, the Christian body, would be lifted up until they would realize their privilege in Christ Jesus. Bless God, it is coming.

By the God within, we cast out or expel from the being that which is not Godlike. If you find within your heart a thought of sin or selfishness, by the exercise of the Spirit of God within you, you cast that thing out as unworthy of a child of God and put it away from you.

Beloved, so should we do with our bodies. So must we do when sickness or the suggestion of sickness is present with us. Cast it out as evil; it is not of God. Dominate it! Put it away! It is not honoring to Jesus Christ that sickness should possess us. We do not want disease. We want to be gods. Jesus said, *"I said, Ye are gods"* (John 10:34). It is with the attitude of gods in the world that Jesus wants the Christian to live. Blessed be His name!

Evil is real. The devil is real. He was a real angel. Pride changed his nature. God is real. The operation of God within the heart changes the nature until we are new men, new creatures, in Christ Jesus. The power of God, the Holy Ghost, is the Spirit of dominion. It makes one a god. It makes one not subject to the forces of the world or the flesh or the devil. These are under the Christian's feet. John said, *"Beloved, now are we the sons of God"* (1 John 3:2).

Beloved, God wants us to come, to stay, and to live in that abiding place which is the Christian's estate. This is the heavenly place in Christ Jesus. This is the secret place of the Most High. Bless God!

The Word of God gives us this key. It says, *"That wicked one toucheth him not"* (1 John 5:18). When the Spirit of God radiated from the man Jesus, I wonder how close it was possible for the evil spirit to come to Him? Do you not see that the Spirit of God is as destructive of evil as it is creative of good? It was impossible for the evil one to come near Him, and I feel sure Satan talked to Jesus from a safe distance.

It is the same with the Christian. It is not only in his spirit that he needs to be rid of sin, nor only in his soul that he is to be pure; it is God in the body that the individual needs for a well body. It is just God that he needs.

The complaint of the devil concerning Job was, *"Hast not thou made an hedge about him?"* (Job 1:10). He was not able to get through that hedge to touch the man. Don't you know that the radiation of the Spirit of God around the Lord Jesus was His safeguard? The artists paint a halo around the head of Jesus. They might just as well put it around His hands, feet, body, because the radiation of the Spirit of God is from all the being.

Now, the Spirit of God radiates from the Christian's person because of the indwelling Holy Ghost and makes him impregnable to any touch or contact of evil forces. He is the subjective force himself. The Spirit of God radiates from him as long as his faith in God is active. *"Resist the devil, and he will flee from you"* (James 4:7). *"For this purpose the Son of God was manifested, that he might destroy the works of the devil"* (1 John 3:8). *"Whatsoever is born of God overcometh the world:…even our faith. Who is he that overcometh the world, but he that believeth that Jesus is the Son of God?"* (1 John 5:4–5). The reason people become sick is the same reason that they become sinful. They surrender to the suggestion of the thing that is evil, and it takes possession of the heart.

Sickness is just the same. There is no difference. The suggestion of oppression is presented, and, the individual becoming frightened, the disease secures a foothold. *"In my name shall they* [the believers] *cast out devils"* (Mark 16:17). The believer says, "In the name of Jesus Christ, I refuse to have this thing."

For fifteen years, God has let me move among all manner of contagious diseases, and I have never taken one of them. The devil could not make me take them. I have prayed with smallpox patients when the pustules would burst under the touch of my hands. I have gone home to my wife and babies and never carried contagion to them. I was in the *"secret place of the Most High"* (Psalm 91:1). Indeed, contact with diphtheria, smallpox, leprosy, and even bubonic plague and the whole range of diseases was part of my daily work in connection with the work of the Apostolic Church of South Africa.

"Behold, I give unto you power...over all the power of the enemy: and nothing shall by any means hurt you" (Luke 10:19). So the prayer of the apostle comes to us with a fresh understanding: *"I pray God your whole spirit and soul and body be preserved blameless* [without corruption or defilement] *unto the coming of our Lord Jesus Christ. Faithful is he that calleth you, who also will do it"* (1 Thessalonians 5:23–24).

Consecration Prayer

My God and Father, in Jesus's name I come to Thee. Take me as I am. Make me what I ought to be in spirit, in soul, in body. Give me power to do right if I have wronged any, to repent, to confess, to restore. No matter what it costs, wash me in the blood of Jesus, that I may now become Thy child and manifest Thee in a perfect spirit, a holy mind, a sickless body. Amen.

4

SALVATION: GOD'S BIG WORD

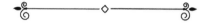

Chicago Pentecostal Convention
July 16, 1920

There is one word in the gospel that is the great inclusive word, comprehending all that God Almighty can accomplish in a human life. That word is *salvation*. In our modern methods of subdividing the varied exercises and graces of the Spirit and Christian experiences, we are in the habit of speaking of salvation in a very limited sense. Very limited indeed in comparison to the broad sense in which the word is used in the Word of God.

I like to think of it as Jesus used it, the all-inclusive word. The one great big word of God that comprehends all that God can accomplish in a man's life forever, from the time He finds him as a sinner away from God, until the day that Jesus Christ presents him to the Father, *"holy and unblameable and unreprovable"* (Colossians 1:22) in the sight of God, until that day when, with our Lord and Savior Jesus Christ, we shall be acknowledged at the throne of God as heirs and joint-heirs with Him and given our place and part in the government of God's great kingdom.

There is much in a man's life besides being "good" if he is to fulfill the large place in the world. God's first purpose is to make man good by removing the consciousness of sin from his soul, in order that he may grow up into God and fulfill the great purpose that God has in store for him, becoming a son of God in mind, nature, power, and capacity to bless.

God's first purpose is to make man good by removing the consciousness of sin from his soul.

Christianity is different from every other religion in the world. Every other religion in the world, excepting Christianity, has no need of a body or resurrection. Their existence after death is purely in the spirit, a spirit existence, but not so with Christianity. Christianity has necessity for a resurrection. The reason for the resurrection is that the kingdom of Christ is not to be in heaven entirely. It is to be in this world. And the Lord and Savior Jesus Christ is to rule in this world. Consequently, while we live in this world, we will need a body like our Lord's, capable of existence here and capable of existence over there.

The Word of God speaks of *"the days of heaven upon the earth"* (Deuteronomy 11:21), when the conditions now prevalent exclusively in heaven are transferred to earth, and earth and heaven become one. These are *"the days of heaven upon the earth."* That is the kingdom of our Lord and Savior Jesus Christ.

And I imagine that perhaps there will be railroads in the kingdom and cities in the kingdom, and there will be government in the kingdom. There will be a necessity for men grown up in God to take places of responsibility in the kingdom. If Jesus was to come into this audience tonight and ask for one hundred men who were capable of taking the affairs of Chicago in their hands tomorrow, perhaps not very many would qualify. Perhaps our capacity would be somewhat limited. Would He find us without capacity to successfully operate its affairs? Perhaps we would disappoint our Lord, and we would be very sad indeed.

The purpose of Jesus is not only to save man from their sins, but by the grace of God to begin in the souls of men that marvelous development in the nature and mind and understanding of God our Father, until by the grace of God we are able to take our place and our part in the kingdom of Jesus Christ and bear our share of responsibility.

I lived in South Africa as a missionary for some years. Among the craving passions of my soul that developed was a longing, awful longing, to get in contact with men of my own race and type of mind, men who understood the things that were moving my soul and had the proper comprehension of the things I talked about, who could also feed my heart with love and knowledge.

When I returned to America, I visited Brother Fockler in Milwaukee, and we talked nearly all night for a week. I just wanted to talk and listen. He could talk about the things my heart was longing to hear.

Then I came to Chicago, and poor Brother Sinclair was nearly worn out, for I was so hungry for fellowship. There was such a passion in my heart to hear his words and assimilate his thoughts and speak out understandingly, such a longing in my soul to hear of the blessing of God and see their point of view. So for almost a year, we traveled from city to city as God led, contacting this soul and that soul until that longing hunger was satisfied, and I felt I could settle down in my own work again.

But you say: "There were lots of people in Africa who were good." Surely, we had many thousand saved native people, and a multitude of them baptized in the Holy Ghost—a wonderful people. But notwithstanding their goodness, they had not been educated in the lines of thought that interested me. They could talk about God, but there were wonderful interests in the world of which they knew nothing, and my heart longed to be able to speak of these things. They were spiritual babies; they were intellectual babies. My heart was longing for companionship on my own plane of life.

Beloved, if God had to exist forever and forever without companionship, the passion in the soul of God would remain unsatisfied. Man came into being because of a necessity in the soul of God. Children are born because of a necessity in the soul of the parents. It is the cry of the real father and the real mother. It is planted there from the heart of God Himself in the souls of man. Every true man and every true woman wants to be a father and a mother and press their own offspring to their bosom and see their own develop to manhood and womanhood and see themselves reproduced and perpetuated in the world.

God is perpetuating Himself in the soul of the Christian. God's heart is being satisfied in you and in me, because by the grace of God He expects us to grow up and out of our little environment and become sons of God and be able to have companionship with our Father. And He will be able to tell us His purpose, He will be able to open His wonderful schemes, and we will be able to take a part and place in the great enterprises of God forever,

Rudyard Kipling, in one of his war ballads, wrote these beautiful lines in trying to reveal this truth:

> And oft there cometh the wise Lord God.
> Master of every trade,
> And He tells them tales of His daily toils,
> And of Eden's newly made,
> And they rise to their feet as He passes by
> Gentlemen, unafraid.

The purpose of the Lord and Savior was not only to redeem us out of filth and sin, but that we should grow up into manhood and womanhood in God and take a place in the world and accomplish the thing that God intended us to accomplish and fellowship with Him on His plane of understanding.

You are just as necessary to God in His plan for the salvation of mankind as God is necessary to you. That is a tremendous statement. I want to repeat it. Christians are just as necessary to Almighty God in order to accomplish His purpose in the world as God is necessary to the Christian. Without God we would not be saved. Without God we could not live. Without God we would never reach a maturity in God. Without man, God would have no medium through which He could express Himself to the world, by which He could minister the Spirit of the living God to the world.

> You are just as necessary to God in His plan for the salvation of mankind as God is necessary to you.

That was the reason God had to send His own Son, Jesus Christ, there being no other competent to take the place of the Son of God. God wondered that there was no man. He "marveled that there were no intercessors so His own right arm brought salvation and His strength upheld Him." (See Isaiah 59:16.)

Jesus was the first *body*. He was the human body through which God revealed Himself to the world. After He passed on to glory, He undertook to bring into being again a new body—not a lesser body nor a weaker body, but a body greater than the body of Jesus, a power greater than the power of Jesus. That is the meaning of the words of Jesus: *"Greater works than these shall he do; because I go unto my Father"* (John 14:12).

PART II

FOUNDATIONS OF CHRISTIANITY

5

THE SABBATH

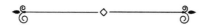

October 6, 1912
South Africa

During the conference, I was asked by the brethren to deliver a discourse on the subject of the Sabbath day for the guidance of the workers. It is not my purpose to deal with the subject in an argumentative manner, but rather in the form of a pronouncement of the position of the church.

The Word of God is sufficiently clear. It has already defined the position for the Christian in the most emphatic way. The second chapter of Colossians is perhaps as clear a portion of Scripture on this particular issue as any portion of the Word. It seems most difficult for Christians to understand and realize, in our entrance into Christ Jesus by the reception of the Spirit of God who abides within, that our Christian experience has been moved into a different place from that in which we lived before.

I have tried at different times to define the operation of the Spirit of God in the different dispensations, in order that we may get a clear basis on which to rest. I will review this in a word.

The Patriarchal Dispensation

In the patriarchal dispensation, God seems to have been approaching man from this standpoint: as if man was far removed from God, and as if God was endeavoring to reveal Himself to man. Abraham perhaps furnishes the best example in the Word, and to him God appeared twice, twenty years apart. There was a lapse of twenty years in which Abraham heard nothing from God. Then, God spoke to him again. Now, that is the best revelation from God to man that is given us in the Patriarchal dispensation, and it seems as if the position was "God Himself to man."

The Mosaic Dispensation

The Mosaic dispensation was different. It was a fuller revelation. It did not destroy any of the revelation of God that the patriarchs had known. God was present with the Jewish people in the pillar of cloud and the pillar of fire, and the *shekinah* over the mercy seat, an ever-present God.

When the temple was built, the Lord abode in the Holy of Holies. In it, there was no artificial light. The Holy Place was lit by candles, but in the Holy of Holies there was neither window nor door, nor artificial light of any kind. The presence of God illuminated the Holy of Holies, the continuous presence of God with man.

The Christian Dispensation

Patriarchal revelation was "God to man," and the Mosaic revelation was "God with man," but the Christian revelation was greater than all. Jesus said in His own words, *"He dwelleth with you, and shall be in you"* (John 14:17). And the revelation of God to the Christian is, "Christ within you by the Holy Ghost," not "to" man nor "with" man but "in" man—man becoming the embodiment of God.

It will be readily seen, then, that our conception and standard must be in accordance with the revelation that God gave to us, and the Christian cannot base his standard of life upon the Mosaic Law in any way. Jesus lifted us up above that standard, as high as the heavens are above the earth.

When the Christian, then, endeavors to go back and live under Christ Jesus and the communion of the control of the law, he has descended from the standard of the Spirit of God abiding within and has placed himself in the same position where the Mosaic people were.

Over and over again, Paul warns us about this thing, and to the Galatians particularly he gives this wonderful warning that, "*having begun in the Spirit*" (Galatians 3:3), they were now going to return to the flesh. And that is the danger with many Christians these days— that, having begun in the Holy Ghost, they might return to obedience to commandments.

The Lord Jesus Raised the Standard for the Christian Dispensation

Someone says, "What about the commandments?" We can see what Jesus says of them in the Sermon on the Mount. In Matthew 5, Jesus said, "*Ye have heard that it was said by them of old time, Thou shalt not kill*" (verse 21). But Jesus lifted that standard miles above where Moses had placed it and said, "*But I say unto you, That whosoever is angry with his brother without a cause is in danger of the judgment*" (verse 22). That is to say, he is a murderer. (See 1 John 3:15.)

Under the Mosaic law, they had to commit an act in order to be guilty. Under the law of Christ, the presence in the heart of the desire is sufficient to condemn. So, in every instance, the Lord raised the standard.

The commandment says, "*Thou shalt not commit adultery*" (Matthew 5:27). Jesus says, "*That whosoever looketh on a woman to lust after her hath committed adultery with her already in his heart*" (verse 28). Jesus took it out of the regime of commandments into the regime of heart experience, and, "*as the heavens are higher than the earth, so are my ways higher than your ways, and my thoughts than your thoughts*" (Isaiah 55:9).

The Great Debate

The greatest debate that has come through these last fifty years between those who contend for the observance of the Sabbath day (the seventh) and those of us who accept the Christian Sabbath has ever been over this one point. Are we still bound by the law, or has Christ made the Christian free from the force of the commandment? And it seems to me that the Word of God makes this as clear as daylight—the Word places our feet emphatically on this ground: that, to us in the Holy Ghost, the law has become a dead thing.

Indeed, it has been spoken of as blotted out (see Colossians 2:14), even that which was written on stone. (See 2 Corinthians 3:7.)

The first chapter of Colossians deals with the history of the fact of the indwelling of Christ. After establishing this fact, Paul goes on to review the subject of our obedience to the law. Commencing with the thirteenth verse of the second chapter, we have the declaration of the expulsion of the law:

And you, being dead in your sins and the uncircumcision of your flesh, hath he quickened together with him, having forgiven you all trespasses; blotting out the handwriting of ordinances that was against us, which was contrary to us, and took it out of the way, nailing it to his cross; and having spoiled principalities and powers, he made a shew of them openly, triumphing over them in it. Let no man therefore judge you in meat, or in drink, or in respect of an holyday, or of the new moon, or of the sabbath days: which are a shadow of things to come; but the body is of Christ.

(Colossians 2:13–17)

Thus far the interpretation is given of the destruction by Christ of the ordinances and laws that were contrary to us, by having established within us by the Holy Ghost of His own indwelling He, having been the Lord of the Sabbath, and we, as sons of God and joint heirs with Jesus Christ, will also enter into that place of dominion, where we too, in Him, become lords also of the Sabbath and every other commandment. Blessed be God!

The New Covenant

Last Thursday, among the questions that were asked, was this: "Do we advocate the partaking of a meal in connection with the Lord's Supper?" And in this thing once again we see the Christian's failure to separate between the Old and New dispensations. For when Jesus partook officially of the last Passover Supper that was ever given to mankind and, by that act, forever closed the Jewish dispensation, there was nothing further to do but make the sacrifice on the cross. And the instant after the closing of that Supper, the Lord instituted a new ceremony, the one we observe today—the Communion of the Lord's Supper. No longer the Passover feast and Passover Lamb, but the Christ of God, who then pledged Himself to shed His own blood for the salvation of the world.

Between these two acts there is as great a distance as between East and West. The one was the mark and stamp of that which was old and ready to decay (see Hebrews 8:13), and the other was the birth of mankind through the shedding of the blood of Jesus Christ.

And so, beloved, when the Christian undertakes that his life shall be governed by commandments, he is going back again into this old life, into the old realm, forgetting his state with Jesus Christ.

It does not mean we shall turn anarchists and that to us there is no law, but rather that we are now obedient unto the higher law, by the Son of God.

The Sabbath Day

On the subject of the Sabbath itself, all the other commandments are spoken of in the New Testament and reiterated, but the Sabbath commandment is not; and that no doubt for this reason—that the prophecies all along had pointed to the Son of God, who was Himself the fulfillment of the law. "*Think not that I am come to destroy the law, or the prophets: I am not come to destroy, but to fulfil*" (Matthew 5:17). For "*the law was our schoolmaster to bring us unto Christ*" (Galatians 3:24). When we got to Christ, beloved, we were beyond the sphere of the law. The law was a schoolmaster to bring us to Christ. Blessed be His name.

So with Sabbath, Christ Himself, the Eternal Rest into which the Christian enters—not to abide on the Sabbath day, but to abide always, every day, and forever—is our Sabbath alone.

When we live in the Son of God, we have come beyond the sphere of commandment, for the law was made for the unlawful and unholy, for murderers of fathers and mothers, for whoremongers, etc. (See 1 Timothy 1:9–10.) Upon our statute books today there are no doubt a thousand laws that you and I know nothing about, and we could care less. Why? They are of no interest to us. We hardly pay any attention to the law of murder, nor can we tell the details, because of the fact that, being sons of God, we are living in love and are not interested in what the law says of murder. There is no murder in our hearts. Blessed be God! We have passed on.

And so the Christian who has entered into Christ Jesus and is abiding in Him and is a possessor of the Holy Ghost has moved beyond the regime of the law and commandments. They are of no value to him. He lives in obedience to one law and one commandment, the eleventh. This includes all the rest in one: "*That ye love one another, as I have loved you*" (John 15:12). Blessed be His name.

> The Christian who has entered into
> Christ Jesus and is abiding in Him and is
> a possessor of the Holy Ghost has moved beyond
> the regime of the law and commandments.

An Apt Illustration

In his book *The Greatest Thing in the World,* Henry Drummond gives an illustration that is so fitting. He says that he visits at a friend's home. He finds that he and his wife have lived together in the most beautiful unity for many years. But a friend of his is still anxious that he should be a strict observer of the law, and so he sits down and writes a code of the rules for the government of this man and wife who have always lived together in unity. He says, "Thou shalt not kill her. Thou shalt not bear false witness against her. Thou shalt not steal from her," and so on, through the other commandments. The man takes it up and laughs. Of what value is such a code to him? Has he not for all the years past been giving to his wife his heart's affection, which makes it impossible for such things to enter his soul?

And there is just that much difference between the Christian standard and the standard of the law. May God help us that we shall not take backward steps, but realize our positions as sons of God. We shall live in Him and abide in the Holy Ghost and realize the freedom of sons, not the bondage of servants. Blessed be His name. Nevertheless, to the man outside Christ, the commandment still stands. As on our statute books today the law of murder applies to the man who commits murder, but the man in Christ has passed beyond that sphere.

Let no man therefore judge you in meat, or in drink, or in respect of an holyday, or of the new moon, or of the sabbath days: which are a shadow of things to come; but the body is of Christ.

(Colossians 2:16–17)

Blessed be His name! Blessed be His name!

Our Highest Christian Privilege

Now, we will never get the force of the second chapter of Colossians—where the Word portrays the exaltation of the Son of God, even to the sitting down at the right hand of the Father in the heavenly places, far above all principality, and power, and might, and dominion, and every name that is named (see Ephesians 1:19–23)—and the second chapter of Ephesians—portraying our lifting up out of the regime of death and sin into the same exaltation of the Son of God—until we realize our high privileges in Christ Jesus.

Indeed, I have this in my heart: The low state of Christian experience that is common among men is mostly accounted for by this one fact—that Christians have failed to grasp the exalted place into which Jesus Christ puts us when we have been made sons of God. May God write that deep in our souls, that we may not keep the seventh day (which was a shadow of good things to come), because *"the body is of Christ,"* not the commandments. But by holy Christian privilege one day is sacred to God, and that without any commandment at all, but out of the gladness of the Christian heart. Blessed be His name! One day is set aside in commemoration of His resurrection, but with the Christian and in the life of Christ Jesus, every day is as holy as every other day, and there is no distinction of days whatever, for the life is in Him (in the Son of God), and He is the same every day. Blessed be His name.

The First Day

But, beloved, have we not cause to rejoice that in Christianity there has been established a day of commemoration of His resurrection, and that all together the Christian world unites in exalting the Son of God by keeping that day holy? We may not let down on our reverence for the first day of the week, but may we as Christians exalt the day not by obedience to commandment, but as Jesus Himself did, by making it a day when His life was given forth for the benefit of others, and I know God will bless us.

Now, I hope that forever this question is settled in our hearts: That, so far as our church is concerned, God has helped us to come together to recognize the fact that every man has the privilege to be led by the Spirit—not to observe all the law but to be led by His Spirit.

The Sabbath

The stone which the builders refused is become the head stone of the corner. This is the LORD's doing; it is marvellous in our eyes. This is the day which the LORD hath made; we will rejoice and be glad in it. (Psalm 118:22–24)

When did the rejected stone become the head of the corner? When Jesus rose from the dead on that wonderful resurrection morning. "*This is the day which the LORD hath made; we will rejoice and be glad in it.*" This is one reason we worship on the day of His resurrection. It is the Sabbath of the new covenant.

A world without a Sabbath would be like a man without a smile, like a summer without flowers, and like a homestead without a garden. It is the joyous day of the week. —*Henry Ward Beecher*

6

BUILDING ON A FIRM FOUNDATION

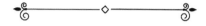

March 1, 1914
Philadelphia, Pennsylvania

Y*e shall receive power, after that the Holy Ghost is come upon you"* (Acts 1:8). We are entitled to it, bless God. We are glad to see some of it and wish, bless God, that we might see a great deal more. And beloved, I have a splendid conviction in my heart that we will. I want to read some familiar verses, as a basis of thought.

> *When Jesus came into the coasts of Caesarea Philippi, he asked his disciples, saying, Whom do men say that I the Son of man am? And they said, Some say that thou art John the Baptist: some, Elias; and others, Jeremias, or one of the prophets. He saith unto them, But whom say ye that I am? And Simon Peter answered and said, Thou art the Christ, the Son of the living God. And Jesus answered and said unto him, Blessed art thou, Simon Barjona: for flesh and blood hath not revealed it unto thee, but my Father which is in heaven. And I say also unto thee, That thou art Peter, and upon this rock I*

will build my church; and the gates of hell shall not prevail against it.   (Matthew 16:13–18)

Those of us who are familiar with this passage of Scripture will remember that Peter is very careful to call attention to the fact that Jesus wasn't referring to him as the one upon whom the church was to be built. He speaks in the second chapter of 1 Peter of how Jesus Christ is the great foundation and is established upon the apostles and prophets, Jesus Christ Himself being the chief cornerstone, etc.

Foundation laying is always a hard process. Over here in the East, with your solid ground, you are not so badly as some cities in the West— Chicago, for example. Chicago is built on a great quicksand bed, which is from seventy to eighty feet deep. After the Great Chicago Fire, the board of aldermen did a thing that no body of men had ever dared to do till then. They passed an ordinance raising the grade of the city sixteen feet. In sections of the city where the old buildings still stand, you go down a story and a half from the street level to the original street. It was a tremendous undertaking, but it got them everlastingly out of the mud. So, sometimes, a destructive process is good. The Chicago Fire became the great means by which the new and wonderful city came into existence.

I want to talk to you today about foundation building. When I was a young man, I was a builder. I looked upon Chicago as the great Mecca for all builders, so I got to Chicago as quick as I could. I looked around among various occupations and settled on this fact: There were two classes of men always in demand—the man who understands scientific foundation building, and the man who understands scientific roofing. And I said, "I will master these two things."

In those days, they used to build twelve-story skyscrapers, sometimes fourteen-story ones. Foundation building was not known as it is today. In those days, they went to the forests and brought great pilings that were seventy, eighty, and ninety feet long. These were driven into the ground until they touched bedrock. At the surface, these were cut off level, and railroad iron was laid on top. Then, they commenced their stonework on top of the railroad iron, and, after they got to the street level, it would probably be brick.

I lived long enough to see that these great buildings would get out of plumb, and it would be necessary for a civil engineer to go over the buildings every three months to see whether they were moving out of plumb one way or another. If they were, great systems of jackscrews were used under the buildings to adjust them. It may surprise some of you to know that some of these great buildings in Chicago would literally stand on a system of jackscrews, which were adjusted every three months by civil engineers. That was too much like hanging a city up in the air, so they said, "We will drive great steel castings down to the rock and we will take out the earth and fill the castings with cement." That system likewise passed away. And now they excavate clear down to the bedrock, four or five stories if necessary. The quicksand and mud are removed. The foundation is laid on the base rock.

> For the church of God and Christian faith to become strong and to be built up in God, it is necessary to get a good foundation.

For the church of God and Christian faith to become strong and to be built up in God, it is necessary to get a good foundation. It is a greater problem with most builders to get the old rubbish out of the way than to do the building. If we will look at our own lives, we will observe this: that the things that have been rooted and grounded in our hearts—some, the tradition of the fathers; some of it, misconception of the meaning of the Word of God, for much of our teaching is fragmented—these form the greatest obstacles to the engrafting of the living Word of God. Every one of us who has progressed in God has found that the difficulty was not in believing the Word of God, but the difficulty was to get away from things that were settled in our own being as facts, though untrue. How hardly have we struggled over the matter of "If it be Thy will" concerning sickness. From our babyhood and all down through the generations, we have been taught that if you are sick, the proper thing to do is to pray, "If it be Thy will," forgetting all the time that the Lord has forever demonstrated and declared His eternal will concerning the subject of sickness by healing all that come to Him.

Well, bless God, some have succeeded in getting over that difficulty and put the subject of praying "If it be Thy will" behind their back and moved out where they believe the declarations of Jesus Christ. So it was that victory came on that line.

Now, dear ones, the thing that the Spirit of God is laying deeply upon my own heart these days is the need of a settled, established state in the Lord Jesus Christ, and the movement of the Spirit worldwide is to bring into unity the children of God who will raise a standard of truth for the world.

Now, listen! This "Come together" call of the Spirit is not an isolated movement. It doesn't belong to a little company of people in Philadelphia, nor in any other city. In the last days, the last months, or the last year, in my correspondence worldwide, I have discovered this quote, and the Lord is beginning to move everywhere in this particular line. Only yesterday I received a letter from Los Angeles from one of the prominent leaders there. He went on to outline the processes of development in God through which he has been brought during the last few years and the final result. I had written of what God was doing in our own midst and what God was endeavoring to do in the establishment of the church, etc. He said, "Brother, your letter is a revelation. We thought that was all confined to ourselves, but I see that this movement, that we supposed was local, is a general movement, and of the Holy Ghost, and it is in your heart just as it has been in ours."

So God is moving in these days on a certain definite line. The man who has a settled, established faith in God has got that faith based on the eternal declarations of the Lord Jesus Christ and is moving in harmony with the revealed plan of God, as outlined for this hour in God's church plan. The difficulty with most individuals and teachers in times past has been that the revelation of the mind of God, as revealed in the Word, was limited to such a degree that they were compelled to take only a certain few of the great principles of the gospel, and thus their entire system was based on them. But in these days, as the coming of the Lord approaches and as the added light of the Spirit has been given, God has revealed in a larger way, in a broader manner, the truth. So that, in these days, it seems to me it is the purpose of God that the church of the latter day, the church of Philadelphia (if you like), should be based upon the great, broad basis of the eternal truth, as laid down in the New Testament by the Lord Jesus Christ and the apostles, not on any fragmentary principles.

In days past, it was thought necessary to endeavor to bind men's hearts and consciences to certain established truths that the church was ready to accept. And so these truths were usually embodied in the form of a creed, and they said, "This is all of truth that we accept. This is our faith." So, they laid this basis and built a fence around themselves. After a while, to the amazement of the church and to her discomfiture, it was discovered that their creeds have been the means that squeezed them in, and instead of being a foundation broad enough for the Word of God, they are strangled inside their unyielding creed, and there is no room for expansion. When the dear Lord has wanted to give a revelation of progressive truth, He has been compelled to go outside of the church fence and raise up a new body. That was because a fence had been built. A certain little enunciation of truth had been collected and the structure established on that instead of on the entire Word of God.

We can see this: The individual who learns truth these days cannot confine it to certain declarations of doctrines. For as the days go by, we see the progressive light of God; and if you were to compare your faith now with what you believed ten years ago, you would find there has been a great expansion. Now, what is ten years more going to develop? What truths will it be necessary for us ourselves to accept from the Lord in the coming days? Consequently, beloved, there is only one basis upon which the church of Jesus Christ can rest—that is, upon Jesus Christ and the apostles and the whole body of truth, as outlined in the New Testament.

Then, beloved, in that great body of truth, there must be the accompanying largeness and Spirit of the Lord Jesus Christ, who didn't confine Himself to certain little dogmatic teachings, but He laid the great, broad principles upon which the whole great kingdom of heaven rests and upon which a great Christian life can rest eternally.

> Jesus laid the great, broad principles
> upon which the whole great kingdom
> of heaven rests and upon which a great
> Christian life can rest eternally.

There never was a teacher like Jesus. He was the one great Mastermind who understood the Spirit of the living God, who understood that all revelation of God was a progressive revelation. And thereby the minds that He must prepare by His own personal teaching were not able to receive all the great body of truth He had to reveal, so He said, "Ye are not able to bear it now." (See John 16:12.) They had to grow up into the place in God where they were able to bear and analyze and utilize the greater truths of the Word of God. Now, beloved, we are in the place, just that place, bless God.

I believe in my heart that God is laying, even in this little company with her one hundred and twenty like the church at Jerusalem, the foundation of the truth of God that will command the attention of the Christian world.

Yesterday I received an invitation from E. N. Bell, editor of *Word & Witness* in Malvern, Arkansas. In April, they are having a great convention down there that includes all the Southern states. Among other things, he says, "Brother Lake, there are two contending forces; the one which desires a strong organization, the other which doesn't want any organization, but desires to be a law unto themselves."

As I read the letter, I said, "They are both wrong." The man who is an anarchist and is a law unto himself and doesn't put himself into line with the Word or cooperate with God according to God's plan is just as great a sinner as the other who comes along and wants to organize the church into a frozen, man-created mass.

Jesus Christ laid down the principles of eternal truth: "Every man who accepts the principles, who lives the life, is acceptable to Me." (See Matthew 5:19.) So, beloved, the church of God in these latter days must just return to the blessed basis that the Lord Jesus Christ laid down.

Beloved, the day has long gone past when men's consciences could be bound with certain little doctrines. If we were to take this audience today, of those who are living holy lives, baptized in the Holy Ghost, and note carefully what this brother believes and that brother believes, we would perhaps have twenty different statements before you got through with this little company.

Don't you see? The thing is this: Our hearts are one in the blood of Jesus Christ; our hearts are one in the recognition of a common Spirit of God. Blessed be His name! Every one of us can join hands and hearts on the seven unities demanded and experienced in the church at Ephesus: "One body, one Spirit, one hope, one Lord, one faith, one baptism, one God and Father of you all, who is above all, through all, and in you all." (See Ephesians 4:4–6.)

So, the dear Lord in these days is once again moving upon the hearts of men that the body of Jesus Christ shall be brought together in holy oneness, that the power of God may be poured upon her, that the Spirit of the living God may move through her in mighty power and demonstration, and that through her the last message of this present age may be given to the world—the great kingdom message. Bless God.

It seems to me we are only beginning to understand with what force the kingdom message is going to come and its revolutionary character.

A few weeks ago, the country was stirred by one man's endeavor to just touch in a small way the first principle of Jesus Christ, that first one: "*Blessed are the poor in spirit*" (Matthew 5:3). I refer to Henry Ford, the manufacturer of the Ford motorcar. He set aside, out of his profit, ten million dollars for 1914, to be divided between his twenty-six thousand employees. He established a minimum wage of five dollars per day to be the wage of every man. Then, every two weeks, he would receive in a check the proportionate amount of the ten million dollars, in addition to his wages.

We say, "Bless God, that is a good thing." That's a starting point. It indicates that some men are beginning to see the mind of the Lord. It is not by any means a fulfillment [illegible]. Then, the selfish man says, "Yes, that will draw to Henry Ford every expert workman in the United States, etc., and his profits thereby will only be increased, not lessened, but it is a start."

Now see, the blessed principles of the Lord Jesus Christ are the principles of unselfishness. That is the one crowning principle that the Lord Jesus Christ wants to lay down in His church this very day. It makes no difference how it is applied. The Lord Jesus Christ Himself didn't undertake to tell us how to apply that principle. He left it to every man in his own station. But, beloved, the demand upon us is that we live that blessed principle of the Lord Jesus Christ.

My thought is this: Jesus Himself didn't undertake to tell us dogmatically how to apply that principle, but He, on the other hand, laid down the principles and left it to us, His sovereign servants, to apply them just as the Spirit of the Lord illuminated our own hearts and told us to do. That is the great basis upon which the Lord Jesus Christ is founding His church. It is based on the principles of the Son of God. He doesn't ask us what we think about this or that petty doctrine, but He lays down the great principles of the kingdom as the essentials:

- Blessed are the poor in spirit: for theirs is the kingdom of heaven. (Matthew 5:3)

- Blessed are they that mourn: for they shall be comforted. (Matthew 5:4)

- Blessed are the meek: for they shall inherit the earth. (Matthew 5:5)

- Blessed are they which do hunger and thirst after righteousness: for they shall be filled. (Matthew 5:6)

- Blessed are the merciful: for they shall obtain mercy. (Matthew 5:7)

- Blessed are the pure in heart: for they shall see God. (Matthew 5:8)

- Blessed are the peacemakers: for they shall be called the children of God. (Matthew 5:9)

- Blessed are they which are persecuted for righteousness' sake: for theirs is the kingdom of heaven. (Matthew 5:10)

Beloved, these are the things that God calls us back to today: to the original basis, to the foundation—Jesus Christ Himself, the chief cornerstone. We see these blessed principles exemplified all through the New Testament by the apostles themselves, who, as the fathers of the church, were desirous that they should not even become a burden on the church and endeavored to keep themselves from being a burden. Who, with their own hands in some instances, labored that they might have the privilege of living and preaching the blessed gospel of the Lord Jesus Christ.

Don't you see, beloved, that every departure from the principles that the Lord Jesus has laid down has weakened the great fabric? Out of that condition have grown our divisions. Our departure from the principles of the Lord has robbed us of that vital faith that was necessary to get answers from God, even for our daily bread. A return to the principles of the Lord Jesus Christ, to the practical life of the Son of God, will bring again upon our souls the blessing of God.

A return to the principles of the Lord Jesus Christ, to the practical life of the Son of God, will bring again upon our souls the blessing of God.

Beloved, that's the entrance into power. That's the final manner of testing the spirit. The spirit must ever be tested by the Word of God, by the principles of Jesus Christ—the law that He laid down by the commandments of Jesus. If the spirit in you won't measure up with the principles that the Lord Jesus Christ laid down, be sure that it is not the Spirit of the Lord Jesus Christ. If the spirit in you exalts itself, etc., just settle it. There is a spirit there that isn't like the Spirit of the Lord Jesus. The way we can see what His Spirit was like is from the principles He laid down and the life He lived.

I feel it this day that the Lord is going to pour a rich and wonderful blessing upon the saints when we come down and return to the blessed principles of the gospel of Jesus.

If I were to advise you to do anything particular during the coming weeks, it would be this: Take the fifth, sixth, and seventh chapters of Matthew and read them and reread them on your knees, until the principles of Jesus Christ enter into your heart. Then, bless God, there will be a good basis laid in your soul for the everlasting blessing of God.

It is as impossible to get the eternal working power of God to appear in a man's life, or in the life of the church, until first the clearing away is done and the rubbish of petty doctrine and littleness is taken out of the way, as it would be to build a Chicago skyscraper without first taking out all the quicksand and mass of rotten stuff. It has got to come out. It has got to be cleared away. When the life goes down on the eternal Rock, Jesus Christ, then the structure will come up and will stand in the power of God.

So this morning I pray God that He will help us this day to take these blessed words of God—the declarations of Jesus Himself as He has outlined them in the fifth, sixth, and seventh chapters of Matthew, especially—and get these real basic things settled in our soul.

I have received during the week applications from several persons who want to come up here and receive membership into this body, who desire to receive the right hand of fellowship. You can't keep it from growing, from developing. But O, beloved, is it going to develop in God, or is it going to be like every institution has been, or is it going to be placed on eternal foundations? And is our life going down into the bottom, to the bedrock, to the foundation stone of Christ Jesus?

Let us pray:

O God, our Father, let our lives be once and forever and for all settled on the eternal Rock, Christ Jesus, Lord God, where our lives shall stand. Blessed be Thy name! And where the church of Jesus Christ shall stand, Lord God, and the gates of hell shall not prevail against her. Blessed be Thy name! O God, let that deep, true, holy, unselfish working of the Holy Ghost in our lives be so pure and true and real that, my God, there shall not be left a superficial thing in us, Lord, but that our character shall be opened wide, opened to the living God, and wide open to one another, O God, reflecting, showing forth, the real life of Jesus Christ. O God, we bless Thee for this day. Lord God, there is an echo of gladness in our soul. There is a shout of praise in our hearts. Lord God, the day has come. Thine appointed hour has come when Thou hast really begun to call together into one body the body members of Jesus Christ whose names are written in heaven. Lord God, we worship at Thy feet, and Lord, we declare our faith in Thee, the Son of God, this very day. Thou art going to bring forth Thy people, Lord God, the church of Jesus Christ, bless God! Who shall give forth to the world the message of the kingdom. Bless God! Who shall raise up a banner of truth and demonstrate a righteousness that men of God will not have to be ashamed of.

O God, we pray Thee, then, that the great virtue of Jesus Christ shall be so inwrought in us that, my God and Father, we shall look with love into the face of every other man. That, O God, our Father, we will have the eyes of Jesus in us and the heart of Jesus in us in such a way that we will not see things that are evil, but that, O God, we will see the good in the man. We will see the purity, Lord; we will think of the things that are lovely, Lord, and that are true, Lord. We will be so pure and clean before God that the light of God and the life of God shall shine in us and flow through us so that mankind will be blessed.

O God, our Father, we rejoice in this day. We rejoice in this hour. Thou art the Son of God, Lord Jesus. We are so glad You have let us live at this time of life. My God, we rejoice in the expectation of Thy soon coming. Bless God! But, O Jesus, blessed Jesus, get us ready, get us ready. Lord God, get us ready to give the message that is going to stir the world. Get us ready, Lord, to receive the power of God that is going to demonstrate Christ to mankind, for Jesus's sake.

O God, we pray that upon this Pentecostal movement worldwide and upon the church of Christ at large, by whatever name it is known, and upon the hidden ones who are known by no name, the power of God shall come. Lord God, once again let the pulsating movement of the Holy Ghost be felt through the body of Christ. Lord Jesus, draw Thy children together. Lord Jesus, establish them on the Rock. Lord God, build up the body, we pray Thee, Lord. And, bless God, we pray that upon our own souls in these days there shall be such a passion of the Christ-heart that we will seek the lost, that we will seek the sick, that, my God, religious life, religious service, shall forever cease to be a matter of religious entertainment. But, O God, make it what Your heart desires, religious service, serving our fellow-men. O God, shedding Your tears with the afflicted, putting Your hands under the weary, lifting them up to God, praying for the stricken ones.

O Christ, let the pure heart and Spirit of Christ throb in every breast for Jesus's sake, that the will of God may come, that the prayer of Jesus Christ may be answered, that we may all be one. Lord God, that Thy kingdom may come and Thy will be done in earth as it is in heaven, Lord, for Jesus's sake. Amen.

7

THE TRIUNE GOD

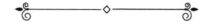

September 27, 1914
Spokane, Washington

Yesterday I knew what I was to preach about—at least, I thought I did—and I was so sure about it that I gave the secretary the subject I was going to preach on, but tonight I do not know. It is all gone. Somehow or other I feel like telling you of an incident by which God taught me the greatest lesson of obedience to the Spirit that I believe has ever come in my lifetime.

If I were in my own congregation in South Africa, I would expect to see a descent of the Spirit upon the people and appearance of the glory of God, manifest in different ways as the Spirit manifests Himself, as I have many times witnessed.

As the days have gone by since I have ministered at this church, every day has brought an increasing consciousness that God has a great and wondrous purpose that He is endeavoring to work out through this congregation.

One of the things of which my spirit is impressed, is that our consciousness of Christ is not as vivid as it ought to be and as God desires that it should be.

God's method for man in conceiving Himself was through the manifestation of Himself in Jesus Christ. And the individual who wants to understand the character of God has only to turn his face and heart toward the Lord Jesus Christ, observe His ways, listen to His words and His Spirit, to know the heart of God.

Indeed, beloved, I have felt, and I feel today, that the world has never had a proper comprehension of the Lord Jesus Christ. We all realize the common conception of the Christ as it has been presented to us by the Orthodox Church at large. And I want to say with all frankness that while in a large measure that conception of the church largely is true, yet it is ten thousand miles below the real standard, or God's conception of presentation, of the Christ as I see it in the Word of God as the Spirit of God has made my own consciousness aware of.

On the other hand, I feel that liberal Christianity hasn't given the Christ His due place, and I believe that God wants to establish a clearness of conscience concerning the Christ in the hearts of men. And this which I desire to say (and I believe not of myself, but by the Spirit of God) is that Jesus Christ was much more than a man. He was the Christ of God, the eternal Spirit.

Somebody says now, "Define the distinction between God and Christ." One of the difficulties that always presents itself to one's heart, and it did to mine from a very early time, was this: It seemed to me Christianity had confused God, and instead of *one* God it had established three Gods. And while in a sense that is true (in the real sense it is true), in the sense it has been presented to the world, mankind has stood facing the fact that there were three Gods. The creed said that they were one, but it has always seemed to be confused in men's hearts how such a thing was possible.

I wish I could refer to other people's experiences rather than my own, but when a man breaks out on a new track, he has no guide but his own heart and his own experiences. So I am compelled in teaching some of these things to refer to personal experiences.

One experience I want to speak of because I believe it will give the key that will help many minds to become clear on one of the distinctions, at least, between God the Father and the Son, Jesus Christ, and their union as one.

I have told you in this congregation on another occasion of how a friend of mine arose one Sunday morning in our tabernacle and presented a request for prayer with many tears, saying, "I have been a member of this congregation for four years. I have witnessed God heal all kinds of people—the lame, the halt, blind, deaf, dumb, insane, etc. And this morning I am convicted of God that I have never even presented a request for prayer for a cousin of mine, who is in an insane asylum in Wales."

Something about the man's spirit touched my own heart. The Spirit of God was deeply present. I invited the congregation to join in prayer as I knelt on the platform to pray. As my heart went out to God in prayer, something transpired within and to me that I can describe only like this:

Presently, my sight and consciousness were awakened to the fact that from this one and that one, from perhaps a hundred divergent streams, faith and power were coming to my spirit and concentrating in me as shafts of light. Indeed, it was the spirit of faith being imparted to my spirit from the hearts of those who knelt throughout the house. An unusual consciousness of God's power and presence swept over me, and presently this seemed to take place, and I believe it did take place.

In my consciousness, I observed that I was no longer in that tabernacle. The first place I became aware of was passing the city of Kimberly. Then I became conscious that I was at Cape Town, South Africa, one thousand miles from Johannesburg. Presently, I remember of the Cape Verde Lighthouse on the coast of Spain, and I remember distinctly of passing the shores of France. I entered the hills of Wales (I had never been in Wales), but as I went over those hills, presently I came to a little village, and outstanding was a building that I recognized as the asylum.

I went into that place, walked straight into the room where a woman was strapped to the sides of a cot, and as consciously as I stand here now, I put my hands on the woman's head and in the name of the Lord Jesus Christ rebuked the insane spirit that possessed her and cast it out.

Her face became calm, and she smiled up into my face. I recognized in the look of her eyes the awakened consciousness.

All the time I had been kneeling on the platform at Johannesburg, and my heart and my voice had been expressing my desire to God.

You ask me what it was—how do I explain it? And I try to in this way. Perhaps I am right. If so, perhaps it will help us in the question that is before our hearts now.

Throughout the Word of God we read many times this expression, "The Spirit of the Lord caught away Elijah, the Spirit of the Lord caught away Elisha, the Spirit of the Lord caught away Jeremiah, or Amos or one of the other prophets." (See Acts 8:39.) Now, that doesn't mean that their physical bodies were transported to another place in all instances, though in some I believe it does. But it does mean that the inner man, the conscious spirit man, was transported for the time being to another place, and he saw and performed acts there.

As quickly as a letter could come from Wales, my friend received a letter saying, "A strange thing has happened. Our cousin who has been in the asylum was suddenly and instantly healed on last Lord's Day, and she is well."

Beloved, I was there. I could tell you to this hour of the old-fashioned brass that was on the door and the pattern of that old Welsh knocker on the door. There was not a detail of the room that I didn't see, and there was not a detail of the trip from Africa to Wales that I was not as conscious of as I was at a later time when I came via that route on purpose, to prove whether or not it were a fact.

Now beloved, I am going on.

In the beginning was the Word, and the Word was with God, and the Word was God. The same was in the beginning with God. All things were made by him; and without him was not any thing made that was made. In him was life; and the life was the light of men.

(John 1:1–4)

And that is the thing that distinguishes Jesus Christ from all other reformers. Varied philosophies have been presented by various minds, but the Christ imparted *life*. "*In Him was* **life**." And the individual today who enters into Christ, and whose heart and soul have touched the realm of God-consciousness that God desires we should touch, received from God, through that open and quickened consciousness, a ministry of *life*—not a ministry of words, not a ministry of inspiration, but a ministry of *life*. "*In Him was life, and the life was the light of men.*"

> Varied philosophies have been presented by various minds, but the Christ imparted *life*.

"*The light shineth in darkness; and the darkness comprehended it not*" (John 1:5). If for five minutes God's spiritual illumination could come over our souls, and our consciousness be awakened, and the things of God as they are and our own relationship to our God be realized, there isn't a man or woman in this house who would not fall prostrate on his or her face before God.

"*The light shineth in darkness.*" It shone then, and it is shining just as brilliantly now.

The darkness comprehended it not. There was a man sent from God, whose name was John. The same came for a witness, to bear witness of the Light. He was not that Light, but was sent to bear witness of that Light.   (John 1:5–8)

Now I will return. Man is the image of God. He was made in His own image. Every function of spirit and soul that we observe within our own souls is but the counterpart of the functions of God.

But someone says, "God has no body. He is Spirit." No, He hasn't a material body, but there is a heavenly materiality as well as an earthly. Spirit itself has a heavenly, or definite, materiality. We cannot define it in the terms of material as we understand it in this world, but consciousness causes us to realize that all things, whether angels or God Himself, have a form of some character of heavenly material.

In my own mind I have tried sometimes to think of what could be the substance of which the person of angels is composed, and my mind has settled on three things as a possibility: light and fire and spirit.

But be that as it may, the Word declares to us that Christ was with the Father in the beginning (see John 1:2), and that through Him or by Him all things were made that are made, and that *"in him was life"* (John 1:4).

And this is my thought, be it right or wrong. I give it to you for what it is worth. The individual who knows everything usually knows nothing, and the man who is sure he knows everything is usually an ignoramus.

My person—my being—was in the attitude of prayer on the platform at Johannesburg, but I was conscious. And the woman was conscious that out from my being something went that carried my consciousness with it, and I consciously performed acts and witnessed scenes that in the natural were impossible. What was it that was transported or projected, for the time being, from my person but the spiritual entity—the real me, self, or ego—in such a degree that it was able to bring back to me all the consciousness that it possessed?

My thought of the Christ is exactly that thing. All through the Word of God we see this. The visible manifestation of God as He appeared to man at different times was in the form of the Christ. I say "as He appeared to man at different times," for the Word records many appearances of the Christ in the world. Once, He appeared to Abraham as he sat under the tree and conversed with him and ate supper with him as a man in the flesh. (See Genesis 18.) The Christ for the time being was embodied in flesh. (See Micah 5:2.)

> The visible manifestation of God as He appeared to man at different times was in the form of the Christ.

Over and over again throughout the Bible, we read of *the* angel of the Lord—not *an* angel of the Lord, but the spiritual entity of God, the spiritual presence of God, "The angel of the Lord."

It would be just as proper to speak of the angel of Brother Fogwell, the angel of Brother Mills, the angel of Brother Grier, or anyone else. The spiritual presence that had power to make itself recognized was present. So the angel of the Lord was the visible, projecting entity of the Spirit of the Lord made visible to the individual.

And my convictions are that the Christ of God, who dwelt in the bosom of the Father from the eternal ages, and who has been presented to us usually as one who came to earth to mollify the anger of God against man [this was not finished]. And the thought has usually been that the Christ is moving the heart of the Father toward mankind. Why, bless your loving hearts! The Father's heart did not need any moving toward the heart of man. For Jesus Christ, instead of *moving* the heart of the Father, was the *movement* of God in behalf of mankind. *"He gave his only begotten Son"* (John 3:16). And the Christ who moved out of God and was present with mankind, in my conviction before God, was the spiritual entity of God Himself.

Then you say, "How can you then explain the Spirit, the Holy Spirit, as separate from the Christ?" And I reply that from your person and mine at this present moment there is a continual radiation of the Spirit of God going on. We feel the conscious presence of the Spirit. We realize the influence of the Spirit. We are conscious of that Spirit passing from our person, not in the form of an entity that carries our consciousness with it or any part of our consciousness, but the simple radiation from within going out.

So God, by the Holy Spirit, is universally present in all the world everywhere.

Way back when the Catholic Church divided into the Eastern and Western branches of the church, they separated over this issue: whether the Holy Spirit proceeded from the Father or whether He proceeded from the Father and the Son. It has just been such foolish questions as this that have interested ecclesiastic minds from times immemorial.

Beloved, no truer word was ever spoken in the world than the pastor of this church spoke this morning, when he said, in substance, "The individual who knows himself knows God." For every function of our being is the counterpart of God and beyond question in a degree that our consciousness has never realized. We are the image of God in truth.

> Every function of our being is the counterpart of God and beyond question in a degree that our consciousness has never realized.

So God the Father, God the Son, and God the Holy Spirit are one God, bless God, just as my person, the entity that proceeds from me, and the influence that radiates from my being is one man—spirit and soul and body. Bless God.

A further word—each one is conscious of our own personality to this extent: at least in our material consciousness, our earth consciousness, we are aware of our environments and the things that take place about us. And through the sensory organs we are brought into harmony with the world about us. All our life and being is on that plane to a great extent, without realizing as we should that the spiritual man and the real man—the God-man, the indestructible, eternal man, the God in us—has a being, a consciousness, and spiritual sensory organs, just the same as our material man has.

The soul is the consciousness, the ego, by which either that which takes place in the natural or that which takes place in the spiritual is brought to us and understood by us.

What, then, can be the greatest awakening that can come to the human heart? Is it not when the clouds are driven back and the soul becomes aware that he is linked to God, that he is a part of God, and that he came out of God? How different our five senses would be if our spiritual nature was developed on the material so that the things of the Spirit were coming to us as they should, with just as much ease as the things of the natural come to us.

When our fellowship should and could be with the angels of God, with the spirits of just men made perfect, with the things of heaven, what a world this would be! People talk about the heaven they are going to, but I want to tell you that heaven is right here when the consciousness is awakened to comprehend and understand and realize what our environment in the Spirit is.

One day, in a time of darkness and distress, as men speak of distress—a time of great strain, but a time that I look back to as the most marvelous of all my life, when, for weeks and months, I walked in the consciousness of the presence of God, so that when I would lie down and relax my spirit instantly would raise into the realms of God—I was walking through the veldt[4] with my eldest daughter and another young lady when an awe of the presence of God overshadowed me, and

4. *veldt*: the open country bearing few bushes or shrubs, especially in South Africa.

I realized God wanted to manifest Himself to me. So I hurried on to the house and went quickly upstairs and threw myself on the bed, giving myself up to my spiritual reverie. In a moment, in the twinkle of an eye, the heavens seemed to open before me, and there was a choir of angels who sang the most soul-ravishing song that my soul ever listened to. And, whether you believe it or not, I declare before God that among that chorus of angels there was one voice that I had known and loved on earth. Those soprano notes were unmistakable. I had heard them on earth, but that voice had a new radius. Heaven is not far away.

Paul said concerning his own personal experience,

> *I knew a man in Christ above fourteen years ago, (whether in the body, I cannot tell; or whether out of the body, I cannot tell: God knoweth;) such an one caught up to the third heaven. And I knew such a man, (whether in the body, or out of the body, I cannot tell: God knoweth;) how that he was caught up into paradise, and heard unspeakable words, which it is not lawful for a man to utter.*
> (2 Corinthians 12:2–4)

God is not far away. God is right here. Angels are not far away, only our eyes need to be opened to see them.

The incident I am about to relate I have on the testimony of three men whose testimony would be received anywhere on earth on any matter of general knowledge.

A little meeting was going on in a little native tabernacle in South Africa. I was not there, but three other white men were present. One of them was Brother _____ from Los Angeles, California. Another gentleman was a businessman from Johannesburg, Mr. _____, a Christian gentleman. But the third was a man whose name is Harry _____, a hardheaded businessman, as keen as a razor, a man not given to spiritual life at all, as we understand it, but a man who was seeking God. His heart was hungry.

Some hundreds of native children were in prayer. (And if you ever saw a company of native children in prayer, you would understand what real prayer is, bless God.) As these children prayed, they said a company of white angel children commenced to file into the church. And they stood in a line all around the wall as they sang, "*Suffer the little children and forbid them not, to come unto Me, for of such is the kingdom of heaven*" (Mark 10:14). When they had finished the song, they filed out again, and one brother said, "I went to the door and stood and looked until they vanished." They seemed to vanish at a distance of one hundred and fifty feet from the church.

You tell me that the kingdom of heaven is a long piece off? Not so. It is right here. It is here tonight. The Spirit of God is as consciously present here in this room tonight as it was on the Day of Pentecost. God is as desirous to pour out His Spirit upon this congregation as He was upon the hundred and twenty of Jerusalem.

I say from the bottom of my heart that I have a conviction that almighty God wants to pour His Spirit upon this congregation and give this old world a new demonstration of the love and power of God.

> We turn our eyes with gladness to the Christ who lived two thousand years ago, but we turn our faces with rejoicing to the Christ who we see living in men's lives today.

We turn our eyes with gladness to the Christ who lived two thousand years ago, but we turn our faces with rejoicing to the Christ who we see living in men's lives today. Right now, God's purpose is that the Christ shall be manifested through every man and every woman, bless God, and that we will realize that in God, in Christ, our union with Him as our elder Brother is a fact, bless God, and that He was one manifestation of God to the world, and we are another manifestation of God to the world. Bless God.

Interpretation of a Message in Tongues

Let the Word of God enter into your hearts with all fullness. Do not be deceived, for God is not only in heaven above, but He is in the earth beneath. The Spirit of God is permeating everybody, every spirit, every soul of man that will admit Him.

Let the Word of God enter into your hearts at this time, so that He may get the glory and the praise therefore. Let the Word of God settle down in your hearts and your minds.

Be not constrained by the evil spirit to turn away from that just God, but be constrained to enter into the fullness of God. Do not be afraid of the manifestation of the Spirit, whether it be in humility or whether it be for raising up.

Prayer

O God, in this hour we lift our hearts to Thee. We are little children and we desire to know God. Not many of us want to pay the price. But, our Lord, we feel tonight that there is a new desire in all our hearts and a new yearning that God should have all our life, and that mankind should have all of God in us. Amen.

8

THE PLATFORMS OF JESUS

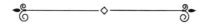

January 24, 1915

There has always been a passage in the Declaration of Independence that has rung very deeply in my spirit. It was the thought of the revolutionary fathers in giving an explanation and reason to the world for undertaking to set up a new government among the families of nations. They said something like this: "Out of due respect for mankind, we feel it necessary to give a reason for such an act."

As we invite this company of people together in this section of country, I feel that a due word of loving explanation may be helpful.

I have been in this particular manner of ministry for many years. I believe Brother Fogwell and I began in this ministry some sixteen or seventeen years ago, or thereabouts. Of course, we had been Christian ministers before that, but at that period God enlarged our vision of Himself and His purposes.

Personally, I received my ministry in the gospel of healing through John Alexander Dowie, a man whom I have loved with all my soul. And though in his later life he became broken in mind and committed many foolish things so that discredit for a time was brought upon his work, yet I knew him from the beginning until the day of his death. I have gone to his grave since I have returned to this land, and as I have thought over that wonderful life, I have prayed in the silence of the nighttime, "Lord God, endue me with the Spirit of God in the measure that You did in his life."

I have always regarded it as a privilege in my life and as a unique thing that, after his death, I was invited to preach in his pulpit, and I preached there for several months. I remember as I stood on the platform, above my head was a great crown, possibly eight feet in diameter. It was made from boots with iron stirrups on them, thick soles, and all that character of thing, that had come from people who had been healed of short limbs. I stood in that place and looked around those walls and saw plaster-of-Paris casts fastened on the walls, some of which had come off of my own friends who had been healed. There were iron braces that cripples had worn and cots on which the dying had been brought, one of them Amanda Hicks.

That cot was fastened to one of the walls above the gallery. I thought of that day when she was carried in practically dead and that old man prayed for her and she was healed. And the company of her students who had lovingly escorted her to the station at Berea, Kentucky, said to me, "We carried her as we would if she had been dead, as pallbearers, and we received her back as from the dead."

Her friends cabled her and telegraphed her from all over the earth, and she gladly told the story, the wonderful story—almost the same character of story that our Brother Zienke told you this morning of the love of God, of the tenderness of the Christ that mankind has not known, of Jesus the Healer still.

Beloved, there is a deep, passionate yearning in my soul that above all else this congregation may set forth, to the praise of God, such a character of righteousness in God, such a purity of holiness from God, that this people may not only be recognized in this city but throughout the world as a people among whom God dwells.

Beginning this work, as I do at this time, I want to say that I do not come as a novice to this time of my life. God has permitted me in the years that are past to assist in the establishment of two great works of God, each of them on a new plane in God. I trust, blessed be His name, that in calling together once again the people of God, it shall be to establish a work on a new plane—indeed, a higher one than our souls have ever known, where the radiant purity of the holiness of God shall be shed forth into the whole world. And I believe that is God's purpose.

Jesus Himself stood at Nazareth on an almost similar occasion. He had been raised in one of the country towns. He had disappeared from His community, gone down to the Jordan, and been baptized of John. The Holy Ghost had come upon Him, and He had returned to His own hometown, to the synagogue where He had worshipped as a boy.

One thing I have always praised God for is that when God put me into public ministry, He made me start in the very town, in the very community, next door to the very home, where I had been raised. When a man fights out the battles of life in his own community—in his own hometown, among his own friends and neighbors—and receives love and confidence, I always feel he has received a good preparation for the next step in life. Jesus knew the place for a man to begin to serve God when He had said to the demoniac of Gadara, who was delivered, *"Go home to thy friends, and tell them how great things the Lord hath done for thee"* (Mark 5:19).

If your wife does not know you are a Christian, nobody else will be likely to, and if your husband does not know you are a Christian, it is a poor testimony. It is the woman who is with you, who eats with you and sleeps with you, who will know whether you are a child of God or not. It is the person who lives in the same house with you and the people in your community who will know best how much of the life of God radiates from your own soul.

It is the person who lives in the same house
with you and the people in your community
who will know best how much of the life of
God radiates from your own soul.

So Jesus once stood in His own hometown of Nazareth and read this wonderful text that I am going to read this morning. It is known, or ought to be, as the platform of Jesus Christ.

The First Plank in the Platform of the Gospel of Jesus of Christ

The Spirit of the Lord is upon me, because he hath anointed me to preach the gospel to the poor.   (Luke 4:18)

Jesus Christ has an anti-poverty program. That is the first duty of every child of God and every church of God that ever came into existence. And the church that fails in that duty to mankind has failed in the first principle and has denied the first platform of the platform of the Son of God.

My heart has never gone out in sympathy to a body of Christian people who have become a little clique and represent a certain select number of society. My conception of the real church of God is one where rich and poor, bless God, alike feel at home, where there are no barriers and no boundaries, but where soul flows out to soul and, in the larger life, man knows only man and God. Blessed be His precious name.

"*He hath anointed me to preach the gospel to the poor.*"

The ministry of the things of God must ever be without money and without price. My soul could never descend to the place where charges are made for the services of the minister of Christ. Never, bless God!

It is our privilege to make possible a ministry to the people without money and without price, bless God. The magnanimity of the Lord Jesus Christ has stood out as a blessed and wonderful feature in all His ministry. I have sometimes wondered how many people really knew how the Lord existed during His own earth life. The Word of God gives us one little hint in these words: *"Joanna the wife of Chuza Herod's steward, and Susanna, and many others, which ministered unto him of their substance"* (Luke 8:3). That was how the Son of God was able to minister without money and without price to mankind. We today may have that privilege, too. It is ours. I have faith in God. This church will demonstrate Christ's ministry to the poor.

For ten years, God has privileged me to preach the gospel without salary, without collections. I never asked a man for a cent in my life, and I have lived, bless God, and been able to minister every day. God has met me every time, and I believe He will meet every other man and woman who will likewise put his or her trust in God and go forward.

The Second Plank in the Platform of the Gospel of Jesus of Christ

He hath sent me to heal the brokenhearted."　　　　(Luke 4:18)

There are lots of them. I tell you, since I have been in Spokane, the Lord has let me into the homes of the rich and poor, and it is not in the poor districts that you find all the brokenhearted, by any means. *"He hath sent me to heal the brokenhearted"*—that is the ministry of this body. If there is a brokenhearted soul in your locality, you are the one who, in the name of Jesus Christ, has the privilege of ministering in the things of God to that soul—brokenhearted sometimes because of sin, brokenhearted sometimes because of sickness, brokenhearted sometimes because of the conditions around him that he seems unable to control.

When I see the living God, in His tender mercy, touch one and another and make them whole—whether in spirit, in soul, or in body—I rejoice equally in either case, for what God does is always good and worthy of praise. I regard the healing of a man's body to be just as sacred as the healing of his soul. There is no distinction. Jesus made none. He provided a perfect salvation for mankind—all that man needed for spirit, soul, or body.

> I regard the healing of a
> man's body to be just as sacred
> as the healing of his soul.

So this ministry, bless God, will be a healing ministry. This church will be a healing church. This will be a church, bless God, to which you can invite your friends who are ill and bring them here and help them. I trust after a time we will be able to bring the people in great numbers—the sick who are on cots and stretchers and crutches—that the Lord Jesus, through this church and its ministry, may make them well.

It is my purpose that a number of brethren who have had this same burden on their hearts for many years, as I have had it, may come together in this city as a headquarters, and that from this city we may extend this ministry throughout the land. I have particularly invited my old preaching partner, Brother Cyrus B. Fockler of Milwaukee; my dear, precious brother, Archibald Fairley, of Zion City; a prophet of God and one of the anointed of the Lord, Brother (Rev.) Bert Rice of Chicago; my dear Brother (Rev.) Charles W. Westwood, of Portland, Oregon; and Reverend Fogwell to assist me in this ministry. Brother Westwood visited with me a few days and is now going on to Chicago to make the necessary arrangements.

This is the outline so far, as God has made it clear. This is to be a healing church. Everyone who has been called to this ministry and those who will be called in the future will minister to body and soul and spirit through the Lord Jesus Christ.

The Third Plank in the Platform of the Gospel of Jesus Christ

He hath sent me…to preach deliverance to the captives.

(Luke 4:18)

How many there are! One day not long ago, I received a telephone call from a lady in one of the missions saying that she had a man there who was a terrible drunk. Every once in a while, he would get delirium tremens. And, at that time, he seemed to be in a condition of delirium.

He saw devils. He was haunted by them. The lady said, "We cannot do anything for him. We thought perhaps you could help him." He came up to the church to see me. He sat down to tell me about himself. Right away I could discern that he was a soul who from his very birth had been gifted with spiritual sight. But instead of associating in the spirit with angels, with God, with Christ, according to the condition of his own heart, all his spiritual association was with devils, demons, and horrors, until he told me that to escape from that condition, he had become a drunk in his youth. In order to have relaxation for a time, he had paralyzed himself with drink, and that was his difficulty.

I said to him, "My son, kneel down. We are going to pray to God." And I prayed that God would bind every last demon and lift his soul into union with God and fill him with the Holy Ghost, so he might associate with the angels of God, become a new man in Christ, and fellowship with the Holy Spirit.

In a few days, he returned and said, "O, brother, it is all so new, so different. As I walk along the street, there are no more demons, no more devils. But as I came up to the church today, an angel so beautiful, so sweet, so pure, walked by my side. And, brother, there He is now, and He has wounds on His hands and on His feet." But my eyes were dim; I could not see Him. I presume they were like the eyes of the servant of Elisha. (See 2 Kings 6:15–17.) They need to be opened. *"To preach deliverance to the captives,"* and more than captives. All kinds of powers, earthly and sensual, bless God. It is the privilege of the real church to bring deliverance to the captives of sin, of disease, of death, and of hell—not only proclaiming the message of deliverance, but exercising the power of God to set them free.

The Fourth Plank in the Platform of the Gospel of Jesus Christ

Recovering of sight to the blind.   (Luke 4:18)

Among the blessed healings of the past few weeks is one dear soul who is not yet completely healed, a blind woman, whose eyes have gradually opened day by day from the first morning of prayer, and who will be present with us in the near future, as Brother Zienke was this morning, to praise God for her deliverance.

"*Recovering of sight to the blind.*" But there are many blind hearts, blind minds, blind souls, just as well as blind eyes, who do not see the beauty and power of the things of Christ. And to them we bring today the message of our Christ, "*Recovering of sight to the blind.*"

I pray that above every other thing, this church will be a church that will know God so intimately that when men come in contact with any one of us, they will feel that they have met one who is able to reveal the Lord Jesus Christ to them. I believe it will be so.

The Fifth Plank in the Platform of the Gospel of Jesus Christ

To set at liberty them that are bruised.   (Luke 4:18)

There are the bleeding ones, the bruised ones, those who have been hid away, and those whose lives have been made a burden. May I tell you this incident?

The last night I preached in my tabernacle in Johannesburg, they brought a young man with whom life had gone so very hard. He had lost hope and gone into despair so deep that he tried to blot himself out by committing suicide. He shot himself in the mouth, and the bullet came out the back of the head, strangely, without killing him. This left him with a violent pain in the base of the brain that caused him to suffer untold agony, and his neck was rigid.

This night, the greatest part of the congregation was composed of Cornish miners, whom I have always regarded as the hardest men I have ever met in South Africa. They live a very hard, terrible life there, dissipated terribly.

This man came up on the platform to be prayed for, and I wanted the sympathy of the people. So I made a plea in some such words as these: "Here is a poor fellow with whom life has gone so hard that he tried to blot himself out, and, in his endeavor to do so, he shot himself, with the result that he is in the condition you see him in now." Presently, I began to observe that up from the audience there came a wave of warm, loving sympathy. I said, "If you have never prayed in your life, if you have never prayed for yourself, bow your head and pray tonight, and ask God to deliver your fellow man."

I put my hands on him and prayed, and the power of God came down upon him, and instantly the joints became loose, the neck became pliable, and the pain was gone. Looking up into my face, he said, "Who did that?"

I said, "That was the Lord Jesus Christ."

Dropping on his knees before me, he said, "Brother, show me how to find that Christ. I want to know Him."

Down in the audience that night was one of the most cultured gentlemen it has ever been my privilege to know, Lord _____ of London. He rose in his seat, and, reverently raising his hands, he said, "My Lord and my God." He had not been a Christian, but he saw a new vision of the love of God for man that night.

Way back in the audience, another soul was touched. He was a different type of man. He came from a different environment. He rose up

and slapped himself on the hip and shouted, "Bully for Jesus!" It came
out of the depth of his soul.

Beloved, it is my conviction that the purity of Jesus Christ and the
radiant holiness and the power of God will manifest Christ alike to the
cultured and the uncultured, for both hearts are hungry when they see
the living Christ.

> The purity of Jesus Christ and the
> radiant holiness and the power of God
> will manifest Christ alike to the cultured
> and the uncultured, for both hearts are
> hungry when they see the living Christ.

The Sixth Plank in the Platform of the Gospel of Jesus Christ

To preach the acceptable year of the Lord.　　　　(Luke 4:19)

Not next year, not in five years, not when you die, but a present salvation, a present healing, for spirit and soul and body. All you need, bless
God, is to bring your whole being into perfect harmony with the living
God, so that the Spirit of God radiates through your spirit, radiates
through your mind, and radiates likewise through your body. Blessed
be His name.

Among the most precious privileges that is given to the real church
is to be in fact, not in word alone, the body of Christ. The Word of
God speaks of "the church," which is His body. God the Father manifested Himself through that one beautiful, holy, purified body of Jesus
Christ in such a manner, such a perfect manner, that when men looked
upon Him they did not see the man Jesus, but they saw God. Until He

ascended and sent His Spirit to the world, to the church, to you and to me. What for? That the new body should come forth, and the church, the real church—united to God, filled with the Holy Ghost, whose names are written in the Lamb's Book of Life—are the body through which God is going to manifest Himself to mankind again.

> God has given us the exalted privilege of being co-laborers together with Him.

When God wants to heal a person, the healing does not fall down from heaven, but it does come through the medium of the child of God. Therefore, God has given us the exalted privilege of being co-laborers together with Him. And among our high privileges is to radiate, to give forth from the love-passion of our souls, the courage and strength to help other souls to come to God. And the business of the church is to be a savior, or saviors, for the Word of God says, "There shall be saviors in Zion." (See Obadiah 21.) That is those, bless God, in such union with God that they are able to lift mankind up to the *"Lamb of God, which taketh away the sin of the world"* (John 1:29).

What Must I Do to Be Saved?

Probably the simplest way is to pray, "Father, forgive me all my sins. I take Thy Son, Jesus Christ, to be my personal Savior. I invite You to come and live in my heart."

"Will God hear me?" you may ask. God has commanded all men everywhere to repent. (See Acts 17:30.) Certainly He will hear and accept you, for you are obeying His own command. Jesus said in John 6:37, *"Him that cometh to me I will in no wise cast out."* It is God's will that all come to repentance. (See 2 Peter 3:9.) He is able to save to the uttermost all that come unto God by Him—that is, by Jesus Christ. (See Hebrews 7:25.) What happens to your sins and iniquities? *"And their sins and iniquities will I remember no more"* (Hebrews 10:17). What love God is willing to bestow on us! For God so loved the world—including you—that He gave His only begotten Son for you and for me. (See John 3:16.) Why not bow and repeat from your heart that simple prayer this very moment? It will revolutionize your life and give you that more abundant life (see John 10:10) and the *"peace of God, which passeth all understanding"* (Philippians 4:7). God bless you.

If I were to come as an accredited agent to you from the upper sanctuary, with a letter in invitation to you, with your name and address on it, you would not doubt your warrant to accept it. Well, here is the Bible, your invitation to come to Christ. It does not bear your name and address; but it says, "Whosoever"—that takes you in. It says, "All"—that takes you in. It says, "If any"— that takes you in. What can be surer and freer than that?

—*Dr. Chalmers*

The depths of our misery can never fall below the depths of mercy. —*Sibbes*

"Watch ye, stand fast in the faith, quit you like men, be strong" (1 Corinthians 16:13). *"Be strong in the Lord"* (Ephesians 6:10). *"Be strong in the grace that is in Christ Jesus"* (2 Timothy 2:1).

True love never grows heavy. Who would be loved must love. Love warms more than a thousand fires. Love rules without law. Love is master of all arts. —*Italian proverb*

God is love.

9

CHRISTIAN BAPTISM

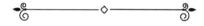

Dutch Reformed Church Hall
Somerset East, Cape Colony

To understand this great subject of Christian baptism, we must view it through its various stages of progressive revelation. For, like the revelation of God to man, baptism has been continuous and progressive in its meaning and character. In the short time allotted to me to speak, I cannot spare the time to read all the Scriptures to which I shall refer, but I will tell you where they are to be found. When the report of this discussion is published, I urge you not only to read it, but to study it carefully and prayerfully, so that this question may forever be settled in your minds. For hundreds of years, many eminent scholars have tried to connect infant baptism with the practice of the male-child circumcision in the Old Testament. It cannot be done; there never was any connection, there never will or can be.

But there is a connection between Christian baptism—that is, a believer's baptism—and the higher, or inner, circumcision of the heart, the cleansing of the natural man from carnality and sin, which the outward circumcision of the male child's flesh typified.

> *Circumcise [purify] yourselves to the* Lord, *and take away the foreskins of your heart, ye men of Judah and inhabitants of Jerusalem.*
> (Jeremiah 4:4)

Again, "*Circumcise therefore the foreskin of your heart, and be no more stiffnecked*" (Deuteronomy 10:16). From this Scripture, it will be seen that God demanded not only the circumcision of the body but also the circumcision (the purifying) of the inner heart-life from all sin.

Now we come to the New Testament. John the Baptist was the last of the Jewish prophets. His ministry crowned and closed the dispensation of the Father. When John began his ministry of baptism, Christ had not yet commenced His public ministry. The ministry of John was nearing its close before Jesus commenced His, for John was the forerunner of Jesus Christ. (See Mark 1.)

Was John the Baptist an innovator? Did he on his own account introduce baptism? Where did his authority to baptize come from? John the Baptist was a Jewish prophet under the law. The common notion that he was a Christian disciple is an error, for Christ had not yet publicly appeared. Where, then, did his baptism spring from? I propose to show you the error of associating Christian baptism with circumcision of the male child.

Error of Associating Christian Baptism with Circumcision of the Male Child

John's baptism had Old-Testament precedent and authority behind it. It is ignorance on this point that has caused the farce of infant baptism to obtain credence and support. Turn with me to Exodus 40 and read. For consecrating persons to the office of priesthood, the law says:

And thou shalt bring Aaron and his sons to the door of the tabernacle of the congregation, and wash them with water. And thou shalt put upon Aaron the holy garments, and anoint him, and sanctify him; that he may minister unto me in the priest's office.

(Exodus 40:12–13)

The Levites were also separated to the service of the tabernacle, from the Jewish multitude, in a similar manner. (See Numbers 8:6–7.) Note that neither the garments nor the anointing admitted one to the priesthood. This belonged to one by virtue of being a priest. It was the washing that separated him from the Jewish multitude and constituted him a priest.

> This separation from the multitude and simultaneous separation from sin by a real, genuine repentance and a wholehearted turning to God were the conditions essential to the baptism of John.

This separation from the multitude and simultaneous separation from sin by a real, genuine repentance and a wholehearted turning to God were the conditions essential to the baptism of John. *"John did baptize in the wilderness, and preach the baptism of repentance for the remission* [forgiveness and putting away] *of sins"* (Mark 1:4). In this demand, he stood only upon the high plane of circumcision (purifying) of the heart which God demanded.

Now, from whom did he demand repentance? From all who would be baptized, though already they, when children, had been circumcised. John himself had been circumcised. (See Luke 1:59.) Again, in Luke 2:21, we read that Jesus also was circumcised. This brings us to where we can plainly understand the reason why Jesus had to be baptized.

Why Was Jesus Baptized?

According to the law, a priest had to be thirty years of age before he could be consecrated to the priesthood. And in Luke 3, we read,

> *Now when all the people were baptized* [Jesus came last, so His baptism was not an example for others], *it came to pass, that Jesus also being baptized, and praying, the heaven was opened, and the Holy Ghost descended in a bodily shape like a dove upon him, and a voice came from heaven, which said, Thou art my beloved Son; in thee I am well pleased. And Jesus himself began to be about thirty years of age.*   (Luke 3:21–23)

John the Baptist was a priest, as well as the son of a priest of the Levitical, or priestly, tribe. He was, therefore, a priest according to the law. He was filled with the Holy Ghost from his birth, which was the anointing and ordination of God. Therefore, by divine as well as human authority and appointment, he was qualified to administer the ordinance of separation to the Son of God. Water baptism was the visible sign of separation from the congregation of Israel to the priesthood according to the Law of Moses. (See Exodus 40:12–13.) King by descent from David, priest through His baptism by John, Jesus was now a royal priest forever, *"after the order of Melchisedec"* (Hebrews 7:11).

We will now return and further consider the baptism of repentance which John administered to the penitent for the "remission of sins."

John did not baptize all who offered themselves as candidates. He refused baptism to the Pharisees and Sadducees. He demanded from them *"fruits meet for repentance"* (Matthew 3:8), the undeniable evidence of a change of heart. Children of Abraham according to the flesh, and circumcised the eighth day, they might have been, but, without the inner circumcision—without real repentance producing purity of life and character—they were denied the baptism of John.

> *But when he saw many of the Pharisees and Sadducees come to his baptism, he said unto them, O generation of vipers, who hath*

warned you to flee from the wrath to come? Bring forth therefore fruits meet for repentance: And think not to say within yourselves, We have Abraham to our father: for I say unto you, that God is able of these stones to raise up children unto Abraham.

(Matthew 3:7–9)

Circumcision was the sign of God's covenant with Abraham. (See Genesis 17:10–14.) The Pharisees had been circumcised as children and therefore claimed the advantages and privileges of that covenant. But the covenant with Abraham was conditional: *"Walk before me, and be thou perfect"* (Genesis 17:1). There was no place for sin; the heart as well as the flesh must be circumcised. "And I will make a covenant with thee." (See Genesis 17:2.) But the Pharisees, like those who depend upon what they call the covenant of infant baptism, wanted to claim the benefits of the covenant notwithstanding that they were godless and wicked men.

John drove them from him, warning them to flee from the *"wrath to come."* Heart purity was an essential condition to John's baptism.

And think not to say within yourselves, We have Abraham to our father [like many today who argue, "We had Christian parents, and they had us baptized when we were babies"]: *for I say unto you, that God is able of these stones to raise up children unto Abraham. And now also the axe is laid unto the root of the trees* [heart-sin, the sinful nature]: *therefore every tree* [the individual] *which bringeth not forth good fruit is hewn down, and cast into the fire.* (Matthew 3:9–10)

We have shown that the baptism of Jesus was His inauguration to the appointment and office of priest. He demonstrated and enforced His priestly authority when He cleansed the temple by casting out the money-changers and gain-getters. (See John 2:14–17.) When the Pharisees questioned His authority, He answered, *"The baptism of John, whence was it?"* (Matthew 21:25). He referred them to the baptism of John as the official act and seal of His separation and induction to the priestly office, which was the "fulfilling of all righteousness" of which He spoke at His baptism. (See Matthew 3:15.) Now we come to the evolution of baptism in the New Testament and there learn its deepening significance and its increased demand upon the life and heart and conscience of the baptized.

The Baptism of John

Into what name did John baptize? Into the name of the Father. John's baptism was by single immersion into the name of the Father only; for the Son, Jesus, was not yet revealed. The public ministry of Jesus Christ commenced only when John's preaching and baptism were at the climax of power and popularity, from that point to decline, to fade, and to pass away to make room for a new development under the preaching and baptism of Jesus.

Let us read in the third chapter of John:

And they came unto John, and said unto him, Rabbi, he that was with thee beyond Jordan, to whom thou bearest witness, behold, the same baptizeth, and all men come to him. (John 3:26)

Read on further, where John said, "*He must increase, but I must decrease*" (verse 30).

Now we come to the evolution of baptism under the personal ministry of Jesus Christ. Let us read in Mark:

Now after that John was put in prison, Jesus came into Galilee, preaching the gospel of the kingdom of God, and saying, The time is fulfilled, and the kingdom of God is at hand: repent ye, and believe the gospel. (Mark 1:14–15)

Jesus required repentance toward God and faith in God the Father, even as John taught. In addition, Christ demanded faith in Himself, the Son, as one with the Father and coexistent with Him from all eternity. Those who accepted Him as the Messiah, the Christ, the Son of God, were baptized by a double immersion into the name of the Father, as were the disciples of John, and into the name of the then-present Son of God. All this only brings us to the practice of baptism as performed during the earthly life and ministry of Jesus Christ.

The Baptism of Jesus Christ

After the resurrection of Jesus Christ from the dead, He initiated His disciples into the practice and teaching of Christian baptism. This is a baptism by triune immersion into the name of the Father and of the Son and of the Holy Ghost. In Matthew, we read,

> And Jesus came and spake unto them, saying, All power is given unto me in heaven and in earth. Go ye therefore, and teach all nations, baptizing them in the name of the Father, and of the Son, and of the Holy Ghost: Teaching them to observe all things whatsoever I have commanded you: and, lo, I am with you alway, even unto the end of the world. Amen. (Matthew 28:18–20)

Here we have a command to baptize into a new name, the Holy Ghost, into which no man was ever baptized before. Christian baptism requires, therefore, from the candidate for baptism:

- Faith in God as John the Baptist demanded from his disciples.

- Faith in God the Son, an indispensable condition to the baptism administered by the disciples of Jesus.

- Faith in God the Holy Ghost, the new name introduced by Jesus into the terms of the great commission in Matthew 28:19, which we have just quoted.

Like the ministry of John the Baptist, that of Jesus had its baptism. Are these baptisms alike? Again, was John's baptism identical with Christian baptism? It cannot be so, for Christian baptism was administered to those who had already received the baptism of John. This is abundantly clear from what we read in Acts:

And it came to pass, that, while Apollos was at Corinth, Paul having passed through the upper coasts came to Ephesus: and finding certain disciples, he said unto them, Have ye received the Holy Ghost since ye believed? And they said unto him, We have not so much as heard whether there be any Holy Ghost. And he said unto them, Unto what then were ye baptized? And they said, Unto John's baptism. Then said Paul, John verily baptized with the baptism of repentance, saying unto the people, that they should believe on him which should come after him, that is, on Christ Jesus. When they heard this, they were baptized in the name of the Lord Jesus. And when Paul had laid his hands upon them, the Holy Ghost came on them; and they spake with tongues, and prophesied. (Acts 19:1–6)

Christian baptism was to be administered in the name of the Trinity—Father, Son, and Holy Ghost—and differed widely in significance from any that had preceded it. In the baptism of John, the name of the Trinity was not invoked.

The Johnaic baptism discipled the people to John. It was a seal of subjection to him as God's prophet and as a sign of their faith in the after-coming Mightier One, who would baptize with the Holy Ghost and with fire. (See Luke 3:16.)

The baptism administered by the disciples of Jesus was the seal of their acceptance of, and subjection to, Him as the promised and now-present Savior of man. (See John 3:14–17.)

It is quite obvious, therefore, that these three baptisms differed in quality and scope. In central aim and in purity, they agreed, and repentance was common to all three. (See Matthew 3:2; Mark 1:14–15; Acts 2:38.) But repentance under Christian baptism differs from the other two, being threefold respecting the Trinity.

I have already proved that between Christian baptism, into the name of the Trinity, and the rite of circumcision, there is an impassable gulf of separation and distinction. When religious teachers endeavor to establish an identity between them, their arguments are unsupported by one honest interpretation of scriptural truth. The whole fabric of such contention is as flimsy as the spider's web, while the earnest investigator is left with a list of specious arguments as groundless as they are unconvincing.

The high character of Christian, or believers', baptism as instituted by Jesus Christ (see Matthew 28:18–20) is best seen and understood in the light of progressive revelation. This is further demonstrated in verses 1 through 6 of the sixth chapter of Romans. We will read the fourth and fifth verses:

Therefore we are buried with him by baptism into death: that like as Christ was raised from the dead by the glory of the Father, even so we also should walk in newness of life. For if we have been planted together in the likeness of his death [burial in baptism], *we shall be also in the likeness of his resurrection.*   (Romans 6:4–5)

The "old man" of sin is buried in baptism, and the "new man" after the likeness and character of Jesus Christ is raised up. Lest we should fail to grasp the high and holy demands of God and be satisfied with less than the experimental knowledge of the perfect work of the grace of God within the heart, which God expects us to possess and for which He has made full provision in the redemption wrought by Christ on Calvary, we will further endeavor to emphasize certain important and convincing facts:

- That John refused to baptize those who had been circumcised under the covenant with Abraham, until they had repented and brought forth the fruits of righteousness. (See Matthew 3:7–8.)

- That, though their parents had been circumcised when children, John warned them to "flee from the wrath to come." They were children of wrath, their circumcision and all else notwithstanding, until they had truly repented and turned to God. John further warned them that unless they repented, they would be "cut down and cast into the fire" as worthless and incorrigible.

- That God demanded circumcision (purification) of the heart, which is a conscious, practical, indwelling heart experience.

- That John demanded repentance from sin and a turning to God, and that his baptism was the seal of separation to God. This is illustrated both figuratively and literally by the form of baptism which separated Jesus into His priesthood, being also that which separated sinners from their sins. (See Exodus 40:12–13; Matthew 3:13–17.)

- That Jesus demanded repentance and faith, and baptized disciples. (See Mark 1:14–15; John 4:1–2.)

- That those already baptized by John were rebaptized by Paul. (See Acts 19:1–5.)

- That Paul declared that death unto sin (separation from sin) and resurrection life in God (conversion and sanctification) to be the import, the true significance, and purpose of believers' baptism. (See Romans 6:1–14.) This will bring us to the place where we can see the tremendous importance of baptism as Christ established it. This is not the foolish practice of sprinkling water on a helpless infant's nose.

The baptism of infants is of man's invention, and a wicked parody of the true baptism instituted by Christ. Literally and figuratively, it is a screaming farce. On the other hand, heaven and earth bear witness to the deep spiritual meaning and significance of true believers' baptism. *"There are three that bear record in heaven, the Father, the Word, and the Holy Ghost: and these three are one"* (1 John 5:7).

The Father is He who gave His only begotten Son for our redemption (see John 3:16); the Word is Jesus Christ, *"in whom we have redemption through His blood, even the forgiveness of sins"* (Colossians 1:14; see also John 1:1, 14); and the Holy Ghost is He that witnessed to our pardon, and to our adoption as sons and daughters of the living God. (See Galatians 4:5; Ephesians 1:5.)

Again, there are three that bear witness in the earth—the Spirit, the water, and the blood—and these three agree in one. The Spirit witnesses that He convicted us of sin. The water witnesses to our repentance and public renunciation of sin—that we have become disciples of Jesus Christ and that, being born of the water and of the Spirit, we have entered the kingdom of heaven. (See John 3:5.) The blood witnesses to the remission of our sins, for the blood of Jesus cleanses from all sin. (See 1 John 1:7–9.)

Oh, is it not sad that this ordinance of God, pregnant with meaning of spiritual worth and significance, should be robbed of all its original sense and purpose and degraded to mean only the outward symbol of a covenant made as with Abraham!

> To the early Christians, obedience to God in baptism meant the forfeiture of the rights of citizenship and of the benefits and protection of the law.

To the early Christians, obedience to God in baptism meant the forfeiture of the rights of citizenship and of the benefits and protection of the law. Secular history records that during the fierce persecution in the reign of Nero, and after the burning of Rome, a Roman officer was present at Christian baptisms to take down the name of the candidates; when this was done, the property of those baptized was confiscated to the State, and they themselves were outlawed to become the defenseless prey of malice, or cupidity, from which the State offered them neither protection nor redress.

They suffered every indignity which the forces of lawlessness and barbaric cruelty could heap upon them. They fought with wild beasts in the public arena. They were butchered to contribute to the enjoyment of a Roman holiday. Paul himself was compelled to take part in a gladiatorial contest, and he spoke of fighting wild beasts at Ephesus. (See 1 Corinthians 15:32.) In the eleventh chapter of the epistle to the Hebrews, we read:

> *They were stoned, they were sawn asunder, were tempted, were slain with the sword: they wandered about in sheepskins and goatskins; being destitute, afflicted, tormented; (of whom the world was not worthy).*   (Hebrews 11:37–38)

May God help us to raise the standard of a true baptism as John did! Let us confess that in continuing the farce of infant baptism, which is one of the errors the Protestant churches have inherited from Roman Catholicism, we have robbed Christian baptism of its dignity and power and deep spiritual significance. Let us nobly acknowledge our error. *"The times of this ignorance God winked at* [overlooked]; *but now commandeth all men every where to repent"* (Acts 17:30).

Let us return to apostolic practice by planting again the standard of baptism as instituted by our blessed Lord and Master. The conditions and blessings attached thereto may be enumerated as follows:

Repentance towards God's circumcision of heart (heart cleansing); separation unto God; faith in a triune God; baptism of the triune man (spirit, soul, and body) into the name of the triune God (Father, Son, and Holy Ghost), bringing in a triune blessing; death to sin; life in God; and power for service; witnessed to in heaven by the Father, the Word, and the Holy Ghost and in earth by the Spirit and the water and the blood.

The question may well be asked: What do you do with babies?

To ensure an obedient, God-fearing race of children, let the parents themselves become obedient to God. Wayward, disobedient, and wicked children are *"a seed of evildoers"* (Isaiah 1:4), the product of parents who themselves refuse obedience to the law of their God. *"Behold, to obey is better than sacrifice, and to hearken than the fat of rams"* (1 Samuel 15:22).

After the birth of the child, the parents in due time appear with their child before God in His house. The pastor receives the child and solemnly dedicates it to the Lord and His service. In this, again, we follow Bible custom and precedent. Let us learn what that means from Luke 2:22:

And when the days of her purification according to the law of Moses were accomplished, they [Joseph and Mary] *brought him* [Jesus] *to Jerusalem, to present him to the Lord.*   (Luke 2:22)

Again, in Mark we read,

And they brought young children to him [Jesus], *that he should touch them* [not sprinkle them, but touch them]: *and his disciples rebuked those that brought them. But when Jesus saw it, he was much displeased, and said unto them, Suffer the little children to come unto me, and forbid them not: for of such is the kingdom of God. Verily I say unto you, Whosoever shall not receive the kingdom of God as a little child, he shall not enter therein. And he took them up in his arms, put his hands upon them, and blessed them* [not sprinkled them].   (Mark 10:13–16)

The parents pledge themselves to bring up their children *"in the nurture and admonition of the Lord"* (Ephesians 6:4), to teach them the Word of God, and to instruct them in the exercise of faith and prayer until such time as they are converted and so obtain an experience in God of salvation from sin and regeneration of heart through faith in the precious blood of Jesus. Then follows baptism as our Lord commanded, at which time they publicly profess a personal and practical knowledge of the salvation of God, their discipleship to Jesus Christ, and that they have the witness of the Holy Ghost to their adoption.

These conditions being fulfilled, they are then baptized into the name of the Father and of the Son and of the Holy Ghost.

Immediate Obedience: A Word to Young Converts about Baptism

Reverend Charles H. Spurgeon, in *The Sword and the Trowel*, alluding to the miracle performed upon Saul when his eyes were opened, wrote:

> One more thing that Saul saw when his eyes were opened was what some do not see, although their eyes are opened in other respects. *"He received sight forthwith, and arose, and was baptized"* (Acts 9:18). He saw the duty of believer's baptism and he attended to it directly. You who believe in Jesus should confess Jesus, and you who have confessed Jesus should gently bestir the memories of those very retiring young converts who are afraid to put on Christ in baptism. You know right well that salvation lies in the believing, but still how singularly the two things are put together, "He that with his heart believeth, and with his mouth maketh confession of Him, shall be saved." (See Romans 10:9–10.) "He that believeth and is baptized shall be saved." (See Mark 16:16.) The two commands are joined together by God; let no man put them asunder. Surely, dear friends, wherever there is genuine faith in Christ there ought to be speedy obedience to the other command.

Our Faith, According to Scripture

We believe in, and preach, the following truths as found in the Scriptures:

+ First: Repentance and its fruits. (See Matthew 3:2–8; Mark 1:14–15; Luke 15:18–21; 2 Corinthians 7:10–11; Luke 19:8.) This embraces the new birth, when one's name is recorded in heaven and one becomes a child of God.

+ Second: Sanctification, the act of grace which cleanses the child of God from the evil nature—the old man (see Romans 6:6) and the carnal mind (see Romans 8:7)—and makes him a partaker of His divine nature (see 2 Peter 1:4).

+ Third: The baptism of the Holy Ghost, the fulfillment of the promise of the Father, the enduement of power for service upon a sanctified life (see John 15:3; Luke 24:49; Acts 2:4–5, 8); empowering for service with an irresistible message, as Stephen, in Acts 6:10. Also speaking in new tongues, a confirmation to the believer (see Mark 16:20) and a sign to the unbeliever (see 1 Corinthians 14:22).

+ Fourth: The full restoration of the gifts to the church. (See 1 Corinthians 12:7–10.)

+ Fifth: Divine healing provided for all in the atonement. (See Isaiah 53:5; Psalm 103:3; Matthew 8:17; John 10:10; 1 John 3:8.)

+ Sixth: The premillennial second coming of Jesus Christ. (See John 14:3, Acts 1:11; 1 Thessalonians 4:13–18.)

+ Seventh: Baptism by immersion (see Matthew 28:19–20) and the Lord's Supper (see Matthew 26:26–29; 1 Corinthians 11:23–29).

We are not fighting men or churches but seeking to displace dead forms and creeds and wild fanaticism with living, practical Christianity. "Love, faith, and unity" are our watchwords, and "Victory through the atoning blood" our battle cry. God's promises are true. Hallelujah! Our motto is: "In essentials, unity; in nonessentials, liberty; in all things, charity."

PART III

LIFE IN CHRIST

10

PHYSICALIZED CHRISTIANITY

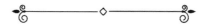

November 21, 1915

The relation of the physical man and God's final purpose has been absolutely left out. My convictions are, and they are deeply grounded, that man's interest in the physical man at this present hour is not a maxim, but the natural development that this present hour of necessity brings to the spirit of man.

Historians tell us that prior to the coming of the Lord Jesus Christ and His birth as a man, there was a strange "looking forward" on the part of man for an event, for the coming of someone who would bring a new light, new life, new liberty to the world. The Jews spoke of him as their Messiah. The other nations, according to their philosophers, had one also whom they were looking for and whom they are looking for again. For the looking forward to the coming of the Christ by the Christian or to the return of Jesus to this world by the great majority of advanced Christian people has spread very rapidly throughout the whole Christian world during the past few years.

There is a reason why the souls of men catch the gleam, at particular times, of a coming event. The spirit that is anticipating and waiting and longing for and believing in the coming of Jesus of necessity has become sensitized along that line and of necessity will catch the fore-gleams of the rising sun. I believe it was that internal condition of the spirit of man that the historians and the scribes speak of as an electrical condition of the minds of men which preceded the coming of Jesus to the earth.

I believe at the present moment there is such a condition in the hearts of men throughout the world being repeated. Men are anticipating. They are looking forward to the event that they cannot explain.

About six years ago, I made a compilation, or rather made a selection, of quotations from some of the great magazines of the world. Among them I remember a statement of W. T. Stead, who is recognized as one of the greatest editors the world has ever produced. He was editor of the *English Review of Reviews*. He was drowned when the Titanic went down. In writing on this subject, he said…. I took the cuttings from his magazine. He had compiled them from various magazines all over the world, experiences that indicated in the minds of men of all classes that men were looking forward to an event soon to occur that they could not understand. However, many felt it. Some even suggested that if there be such a thing, it would not be unreasonable to believe that perhaps it might be what is commonly spoken of as the "end of the age" or the "end of the world."

That "end of the world" expression is a misleading term, for there is no end of the world. There is a new age. And every age has its closing events, and the events are peculiar to that age.

Stead went further than some of the rest. He said,

Christians speak of the return of Jesus Christ, and the establishment of the kingdom of Christ. What events may precede such a thing we know not, but there is nothing unreasonable in believing that perhaps the thing that all feel is produced by the foregleam of the event to take place. Coming events cast their shadows before.

Physicalized Christianity has a reason. It is born because of conditions. It is born because of conditions produced by the Spirit of God, in anticipation of a day when mortal, both the living and those who have fallen to sleep, shall put on immortality. Of necessity men have begun to recognize a physical change that must be accomplished to make such a condition a possibility. Paul, in the words I read to you from 1 Corinthians, says,

> *Behold, I show you a mystery; we shall not all sleep, but we shall all be changed, in a moment, in the twinkling of an eye, at the last trump: for the trumpet shall sound, and the dead shall be raised incorruptible, and we shall be changed. For this corruptible must put on incorruption, and this mortal must put on immortality.*
> (1 Corinthians 15:51–53)

In discussing the subject of the resurrection, he says, "*This mortal must put on immortality.*" Flesh and blood cannot inherit the kingdom of God. Consequently, a change in the living as well as the dead is an apparent fact.

If I were going to give a reason why the attention of mankind is turning to God today for the bodies of men, I would place it right there, in the fact that the Spirit of God or the rays of the coming age are breaking through into the days of this age, and we are anticipating the age which is to come. The very first gleams of the rising sun of that event must discover that it was not in God's will or purpose for man to live in pain, in sorrow, in sickness, and in poverty. But, on the other hand, it is God's purpose and intent of Jesus that mankind should be redeemed from sin, from sickness, and from death, bless God.

No finer phrase was ever coined to express the real thing that the Spirit of God is accomplishing at the present hour than the phrase "physicalized Christianity." The secret of healing, the secret of physical healing is contained in this fact that the spirit of man, in union with the Spirit of God, becomes cognizant of the mind of God concerning itself.

The gleams of immortality that shine into the spirit are transmitted through the soul into the bodies of men, and that is the real issue, the real secret of real healing by the power of God.

I speak of man in the sense that the Scriptures describe him as a triune being—body and soul and spirit. The soul of man has ever been compelled to listen to two voices: The voice of the spirit and the voice of the flesh, or the natural man.

Those who have studied the subject at all of what is defined in the Scriptures as the fall of man, long ago, very long ago, arrived at this conclusion: That the fall of man was the descent of man from the control of his spirit, or God-man, into the control of his flesh, or animal-man. And the spirit became to some extent subject to the animal-man. Redemption is the restoration of the spirit of man to his normal place of authority, whereby soul and body become subservient to the spirit, not the spirit to the body.

> Redemption is the restoration of the spirit
> of man to his normal place of authority,
> whereby soul and body become subservient to
> the spirit, not the spirit to the body.

Physicalized Christianity! Bless God for the phrase. It is splendid. It fills a need. It expresses a pregnant thought, the thought that the hour is coming when, through the enlightenment of the Spirit of God, man has arrived at that place in his growth toward (in) God where he begins to recognize that God has a definite purpose for the body and soul of man as well as for the spirit.

He who works in the greatest calmness, with the holiest and the greatest consciousness of the Father, is he who permits his spirit to dominate his being, not only working with the spirit of man in control of your personality, but more the spirit of man in union with the Spirit of God, whereby the mind of God and the thought of God for this present hour is understood and is being lived up to.

The transmission from the spirit of the thought of God through the soul is a continuous process. The transmission of the power of God from the spirit through the soul and into the body is a continuous process. And the real fact of sickness, the real fact of sickness is simply that somehow a portion of our body loses its correspondence with the rest of our being and is not receiving naturally and normally that sufficient measure of the life of God that other portions of the body are receiving.

The intelligent Christian has long since learned that if a portion of his body is not receiving the due measure of life from God that another portion is receiving, it is because there is not being directed to the afflicted portion of the body the due measure of the Spirit that it ought to receive, and that it is the privilege by the Spirit to take the life of God and direct it to any portion of his body that he so chooses. Blessed be God!

The climax of such thought is not simply the mere condition of physical healing. It is more. Of necessity there must come a condition of health, not healing. And I look forward with great joy and great hope and great expectation.

11

EVOLUTION OF CHRISTIAN CONSCIOUSNESS

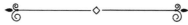

July 15, 1920
Chicago Convention of Pentecostal Assemblies,
Chicago, Illinois

I want to talk to you tonight about my Lord. I want you to get acquainted with Him. Some know Him in one way or another. None of us has reached the place where we have it all, but, bless God, we are on the way. When I was a boy, I thought the sole aim and object of the gospel was to keep from going to hell. A good many other folks observe Christianity from that point of view yet. After a while, evangelists changed the idea somewhat. They began to teach that the object of being a Christian was not to keep from going to hell, but to go to heaven. Then, I began reasoning. I said, "One is just as selfish as the other." The one gets saved to keep from going to hell, and the other one gets saved to get to heaven. Both are wholly selfish, and neither one is the real purpose of Jesus.

Jesus gave one final reason for men being Christians, and, strangely, very few people have ever discovered, even from the Word of God, what that real purpose is.

One day, Jesus came along by the River Jordan when John was baptizing and asked for the privilege of being baptized. John was startled. He said, "*I have need to be baptized of thee, and comest thou to me?*" (Matthew 3:14). Jesus said, "*Suffer it to be so,*" and then He gave the real reason: "*for thus it becometh us to fulfil all righteousness*" (verse 15). In one of the liberal translations, it says, "Unto all righteousness."[5]

Jesus was going to be baptized as His commitment of His body and His soul and His spirit to God forever, in order that from thenceforth He might manifest the righteousness of God.

To manifest the righteousness of God is the real reason for a man's desire to be a Christian—not to go to heaven when he dies or to keep out of hell, but to *reveal the righteousness of God in this world.* And then, heaven and all our rewards will be the natural result of having lived in unity with God and having revealed His righteousness in this world.

God has a wonderful purpose. God's Christian is the most magnificent specimen in all the universe of God. God's ideal for a Christian surpasses everything else in the whole world. Varied churches and varied religious institutions have their peculiar idea of what a Christian is. One of their ideals seems to be that the individual must be able to whoop and hop around and all that sort of thing. But Jesus never did it. He was too big for that. He had outgrown it. We have our ideas of religious meetings. Not one of them is like the meetings Jesus conducted, at least only in a slight way. Then, we have our ideas of what constitutes a real message. My! If you will read the Word of Jesus over again, you will discover that few of our messages are like the message of the Lord. His messages were an uncovering of the soul of man, an uncovering of the nature of God so that men could discern Him, and when they discerned Him, they loved Him. The message of Jesus was constructive, not destructive; positive righteousness, not negative obedience.

---

5. *Editor's Note:* We were unable to find the "liberal" translation in which Matthew 3:15 contained that exact wording.

Jesus gave a new name to God that nobody had ever given Him before. The prophets were intimate with God, and the Old Testament is one marvelous revelation of intimacy with God. They knew Him as a great Governor, as a great Controller, as the One who guided the affairs of the universe, but Jesus knew Him as "Father." He introduced into Bible vocabulary a new name to express God to us.

I am going to talk to you along a line that perhaps may seem new. First, I want to place before you God's ideal of a Christian. Then, by His grace, I am going to undertake unfolding, step-by-step, how men arrive at that stature of Christ.

God's ideal of a Christian is neither a man who is ready to go to heaven nor a man who lives a good life in this world nor a man who has victory over sin or victory over disease. It includes all these things, but it is ten thousand times more than that.

> *And he gave some, apostles; and some, prophets; and some, evangelists; and some, pastors and teachers; for the perfecting of the saints, for the work of the ministry, for the edifying of the body of Christ: till we all come in the unity of the faith, and of the knowledge of the Son of God, unto a perfect man, unto the measure of the stature of the fulness of Christ.* (Ephesians 4:11–13)

And that is the ideal of my heart—that somehow, in God's divine grace, by the wonderful processes of His Spirit, He is going to help me to grow up out of babyhood and infancy into the stature of Jesus Christ. And that is God's ideal for the Christian.

You say, "But, brother, I was saved from my sins." Yes, Jesus was. "Don't you know I was sanctified?" Why, surely, Jesus was. Don't you know Jesus was baptized in the Holy Ghost, but He went so far beyond that it reveals these were but the beginnings by which a Son of God was born and came into being? His development was beyond all that and went beyond all our known Christian experiences.

I want to speak now of the growth of the knowledge of God that took place in Jesus Christ. This will sound strange to some of you. But you say, "Jesus Himself was God." Surely He was; He was likewise man. *"He took not on him the nature of angels; but he took on him the seed of Abraham"* (Hebrews 2:16). *"[He] was in all points tempted like as we are, yet without sin"* (Hebrews 4:15).

He came to our level. He demonstrated in the beginning that man could be an overcomer over the powers of darkness through reliance on God and His Word.

His demonstration began first in the order of nature, where He met no mind but His own. He changed the water into wine by the action of His own will; He stilled the sea by the word of His command; He walked on the water—each one of them an ascent over the other. Each one of them revealing that in the soul of Jesus Himself there was an ever-ascending scale in God.

Then, the next thing in the life of Jesus was when He began His ministry of healing. When He undertook His ministry of healing, He had another *mind* to meet—the mind of the individual who needed the blessing. *"And Jesus went about all Galilee, teaching in their synagogues, and preaching the gospel of the kingdom, and healing all manner of sickness and all manner of disease among the people"* (Matthew 4:23).

Then, Jesus entered a new realm. If you study the healings that took place under His ministry, you will observe that first, it was the healing of disease; next, the healing of the blind; next, the healing of the lepers—a gradual, continuous assent. And last, the creation of eyes in the man born blind. And now there developed in the soul of Jesus a holy dawning of the power of God, even over death, and in His demonstration over the power of death there are three degrees, like the other. (See Matthew 4; 8; 9; John 9.)

The daughter of Jairus was dead for a few minutes. While the father was interceding, the servants came, saying, "Thy daughter is dead." Jesus went instantly to her bedside, and she arose to life. (See Matthew 9:18–19, 23–26.)

The son of the widow of Nain was dead for several hours, and they were carrying him out for burial, when Jesus touched the bier, and he arose. (See Luke 7:11–15.)

Lazarus was dead for four days, and the testimony of his sisters was, "*By this time he stinketh*" (John 11:39).

First instance, death in the first degree, dead a few minutes; next, in the second degree, dead a few hours; and, in the third degree, dead four days; "*By this time he stinketh.*"

My, there is a wonderful revelation in connection with the raising of Lazarus that is not given in the story as it appears in the New Testament. I want to quote from the New Testament Apocrypha, from the book of Nicodemus. It will explain a whole lot to you.

Before I give this story, I want to call your attention to one other thing, because it concludes the thought I had in mind. There are degrees in the experience of Jesus by which He took one step after another in every single realm until He eventually manifested God's divine perfection. There was the crucifixion, followed by the resurrection, and climaxed by the ascension—each one of them a degree in the power of God beyond the other.

If Jesus had died on the cross and there had been no resurrection, there never would have been one single soul saved through the blood of Jesus Christ.

If Jesus had died on the cross, gone into the grave, and been resurrected from the grave only, there would still be no such thing as a real salvation in the world.

But because Jesus died on the cross, entered into death, arose from the grave, *and ascended* to the throne of God and finally received from the Father the gift of the Holy Ghost with authority to minister it to men, there is in existence a divine salvation, sufficient to satisfy the nature of every man.

The Story of Lazarus

In the story that I wanted to bring to you is this marvelous incident. Just prior to the crucifixion of Jesus, Satan appeared in the regions of death and said to Beelzebub, the keeper of the Regions of Death, that he might now prepare to receive Jesus Christ, because he (Satan) had brought to pass such a combination of circumstances that Jesus was to be crucified. Beelzebub replied, "But, Satan, is not this Jesus of Nazareth, who in His divine nature was so strong that He came here and took from our midst Lazarus when he was here, and we could not hold him?"

Satan said, "Yes, He is the one."

Beelzebub said, "But if in His divine nature He was so strong that He came and took Lazarus from our hands, and we could not hold him, how can we hold Him Himself?" That was the problem.[6]

Now I am going back. What is the real secret of the resurrection? That Jesus arose from the dead? No! Lots of men had risen from the dead. Way back in the Old Testament, they opened a grave to bury a man, and when he touched the bones of Elisha, there was enough of the Spirit of God in the old dry bones to give him life, and he arose. But he brought no revelation of God and manifested no particular power of God in the world.

The son of the widow of Nain was truly dead and was raised to life, but he brought no revelation from the dead. Lazarus was dead four days and restored again, but, so far as the record goes, Lazarus knew no more after his resurrection than he did before.

At the crucifixion of Jesus Himself, many that were dead arose and appeared in the city. (See Matthew 27:52–53.)

---

6. The Gospel of Nicodemus, Part 2, Chapter 4, from the Apocrypha. The Apocrypha is a collection of writings considered by most Bible scholars to be uninspired and of doubtful authority. Written between 1200 B.C. and 150 A.D., they provide colorful stories and some historical background.

It was not in the mere fact, then, that they arose from the dead, or that Jesus arose from the dead, that gives the secret of the resurrection. I want you to see what it is.

All the way along in the life of Jesus there is a growth in consciousness of God. Step-by-step, Jesus Christ discerned God and His purpose for man and God's purpose for Himself. Step-by-step, Jesus entered into the truth of His vision. Step-by-step, Jesus revealed the power of God in the new light that had dawned upon His soul until finally, after He had manifested His power in these three degrees of death, ending in the resurrection of Lazarus after he had been dead four days, He began to talk to His disciples about a new problem and a new possibility. He began to open the fact that He Himself was likely to be crucified. In fact, that it was in the prophecies that He should be and in the determined councils of the Godhead.

I want you to distinguish between Christianity and philosophy, for in these days the world is filled with philosophical religions, and everything psychological is used to impress the world that it is religious. And Christians ought to know what it is that makes the distinction between Christianity and philosophy and what makes Jesus distinct from the philosophers, and why it is that Christianity has a power that philosophy has not.

Christianity has a power that philosophy has not.

Some of the philosophies were old and whiskered and ready to die when Jesus was born. The Bhagavad Gita[7] was written eight hundred years before Isaiah. Buddha lived hundreds of years before Jesus and taught most of the things Jesus taught. Confucianism was old, Brahmanism was old, most of the ancient philosophies were old when Jesus came to the world. The philosophers wrote their tenets, left them,

---

7. *Bhagavad Gita*: a Hindu devotional work in poetic form.

came to the grave and died, and their revelation ceased. There was nothing remaining but the tenets they had written.

Buddha wrote his tenets, came to the grave; Confucius wrote his tenets, came to the grave; Brahman wrote his tenets, came to the grave; the Zenclavestas were written, and their authors came to the grave. They all died, and there was no further revelation. The grave ended all.

Not so with the Son of God. Not so the Lord Jesus. Why, Christianity *began* where philosophy left off. The crucifixion of Jesus was but the entrance into the greatest of His divine revelations. Jesus not only rose from the dead, but He determined in His own soul to take captive that power that had been captivating men and subjecting them to death's control. So Jesus entered into the grave. The early church was much more conversant with this phase of the Lord's victory than we are.

The literature of the early church fathers is full of the wonder of what took place in the life and ministry of Jesus after He was in the grave. Peter gives us just two little flashes. He says, *"He went and preached unto the spirits in prison; which sometime were disobedient, when once the long-suffering of God waited in the days of Noah, while the ark was a preparing"* (1 Peter 3:19–20). Next, He went and *"preached also to them that are dead"* (1 Peter 4:6). What for? *"That they might be judged according to men in the flesh"* (verse 6).

He carried His word of testimony and power to the very dead, those who were dead before the flood and those who died between the flood and Himself. There are two classes—the spirits that were in prison from the days of Noah, and He went also and preached to them that are dead, that they might be judged according to men in the flesh. Remember that Jesus preached to the dead. The dead of His day had the prophets to listen to and receive and believe their teachings or reject them, just as you and I have. The purpose of His teaching was that they might be judged as men in the flesh.

Next, in the soul of Jesus there grew that wonderful consciousness that, having liberated them from death's power, there was a step further yet to go. He must take captive the power that was binding their souls.

So He entered into death, and His ministry and victory in the regions of death was the result. And one day He came forth from the dead, a living man once more, as He was before He died.

Over and over again, John tells us that He did this and He performed that work and He wrought that marvel and that in order that we might believe, in order that He might reveal to the satisfaction of the souls of those who were trying to believe that there was a foundation and a reason and a substantial ground on which their confidence in Christ could rest.

So He came forth from the dead with the consciousness of God and His power and His ability to command God's power and utilize it, that no other in all the earth or sea or heaven ever had. No philosopher ever had it, or had ever known anything of it. But when Jesus came forth from the dead, He came forth speaking a word that had never been spoken in the world before. He said, *"All power is given unto me in heaven and in earth"* (Matthew 28:18). Blessed be the name of God! He had proven it. Faith had become fact; vision was now consciousness.

All the triumph of Jesus in the regions of death had wrought in His soul the wonder of God. No other life ever had it. No other soul ever got the flame of it. No other nature ever felt the burning of it. Bless God.

And He was so anxious to lift His followers into it that the very first thing He did after His reappearance among them was to *breathe* on them. He said, "Let Me give it to you. Let Me breathe it into your life. *'Receive ye the Holy Ghost'* (John 20:22)." Let me put it into your hearts, burn it into your soul, establish it into your nature. His victory over death had wrought the marvel.

But, beloved, that is not *Christianity.* Christianity is *more than that.* That is not the consciousness of Christianity. The consciousness of Christianity is greater than that. It was holier than that, more powerful than resurrection consciousness. When Jesus came forth from the dead, He was able to declare, *"All power is given unto me in heaven and in earth. Go ye therefore..."* (Matthew 28:18–19).

Oh, then there were some wonderful days—forty wonderful days in which Jesus took the disciples, who had been in His own school for three-and-a-half years, through a new course. In these days, we would call it postgraduate course. So, they went out into the mountains of Galilee, all by themselves, for a postgraduate course with the risen Lord. And He taught them of the power of God, and He taught them of power over death and the divine fact that the dominion of the risen Christ is for every soul.

David, describing it, said, *"Thou hast led captivity captive"* (Psalm 68:18). Not only that, but beyond it. *"Thou hast received gifts for men"* (Psalm 68:18).

So, one day, there came the ascension. He took them out on the Mount of Olives and, as He blessed them, He rose out of their sight to glory. Then, there is one of those wonderful divine flashes in the Word of God that just illuminates a whole life.

Peter was preaching on the day of Pentecost. The power of God had fallen upon the people. The people demanded an explanation. "What is it? What does it mean?" Peter replied, *"This is that which was spoken by the prophet Joel"* (Acts 2:16). Then, he went on and taught them concerning Christ, took them from His crucifixion through His resurrection and His ascension up to the throne of God. And when he got the people at the throne of God and their minds fixed there, he gave them the final explanation: when Jesus had arrived at the throne of God, an interview between God the Father and Jesus Christ took place. And God gave to Jesus the gift of the Holy Ghost, and the explanation was, *"He hath shed forth this, which ye now see and hear"* (verse 33).

Say, beloved, the Holy Ghost is born out of the heart of the Father God Himself, ministered through the soul of Jesus Christ, the High Priest of God, into your heart and mine. It is intended to lift our hearts and lift our lives out of Chicago mud and to keep us there forever.

So, the real Christian ought to be the kingliest man in the whole earth, the princeliest man in the whole earth—as kingly and princely and lovely and holy as the Son of God—as big as Jesus, with the power of Jesus and the love of Jesus. Bless God.

12

CHRIST LIVETH IN ME

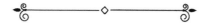

"Christ liveth in me."
—Galatians 2:20

That is the revelation of this age. That is the discovery of the moment. That is the revolutionizing power of God in the earth. It is the factor that is changing the spirit of religion in the world and the character of Christian faith. It is divine revitalization.

The world is awakening to that marvelous truth, that Christ is not only in the heavens and in the atmosphere outside; but that Christ is in heaven and in the atmosphere outside, and Christ is in you.

The world lived in darkness for thousands of years. There was just as much electricity in the world then as now. It is not that electricity has just come into being. It was always here. But men have discovered how to utilize it and bless themselves with it.

Christ's indwelling the human heart is the mystery of mysteries. Paul gave it to the Gentiles as the supreme mystery of all the revelation of God and the finality of all wonder that he knew.

"*Christ in you*" (Colossians 1:27). Christ has a purpose in you. Christ's purpose in you is to reveal Himself to you, through you, in you. We repeat over and over that familiar phrase "*the church, which is his body*" (Ephesians 1:22–23), but if we realized the truth of it and the power of it, this world would be a different place. When the Christian church realizes that they are the tangible, living, pulsating flesh and bones and blood and brain of Jesus Christ, and that God is manifesting Himself through each one every minute and is endeavoring to accomplish His big will for the world through them, not through some other body, then Christian responsibility would be understood.

Jesus Christ operates through you. He does not operate independently of you. He operates through you. Man and God become united. That is the divine secret of a real Christian life. It is the real union, the real conscious union of man and God. There is no substitute for that relationship. You can manufacture all the ordinances on earth, all the symbols there ever were, until you become dazed and you lose yourself in the maze of them, and still you must find God.

Man and God become united.
That is the divine secret of a real Christian life.

There is only one reality. That reality is God. The soul of man must contact God, and unless the spirit of man is truly joined to God, there is no such thing as real Christian manifestation. All the processes of preparation by which a soul is prepared by God for such manifestation are only preliminary processes. The final end is that men may reveal God and that God may not only have a place of residence, but a right of action, in the body and spirit of man. Every Spirit-taught man in the world is aware of how gradually his own nature has become subjected to God and His will.

I was visiting with a gentleman this afternoon who had a grouch on me. He said, "I wrote you a twenty-four-page letter, and you have not received it. If you had, you would not be here." I laughed. That man has been a Christian for thirty or forty years, always a devout man, and I have spoken often of him to my wife and my friends as one of the most consistent Christian men I ever knew. Yet, every once in a while, the big human just rises up above the spirit and spoils the beauty and delight and wonder of the life that is revealing God.

God's effort and God's purpose in us is to bring all the conditions of our being into harmony with His will and mind. God's purpose is not to make an automaton. We see a ventriloquist operating a little wooden dummy, and the wooden dummy's lips move and it looks as though it was talking. He is just moving in obedience to another power.

Now, God has a higher purpose than making man an automaton. God's highest is to bring out all the qualities of God in your own soul, to bring out all the individuality that is in your life, not to submerge or destroy, but to change it, to energize it, to enlarge it, until all your individuality and personality and being are of the nature and substance and quality of God.

You notice among the most devout Christians how continuously their thought is limited to that place where they can be exercised or moved by God. But God's best is more than that. Receive the Spirit, then use the Spirit for God's glory.

While I was in Chicago, I met a couple of old friends who invited me to dinner. At dinner, the lady, who is a very frank woman, said, "Mr. Lake, I have known you so long and have had such close fellowship for so many years, I am able to speak perfectly frankly."

I said, "Yes, absolutely."

"Well," she said, "there is something I miss about you. For lack of words, I am going to put it in Paul's words: *I bear in my body the marks of the Lord Jesus*' (Galatians 6:17). You do not seem to have the marks of Jesus."

I said, "That depends whether or not it is the marks or mannerisms. If you are expecting that the personality God gave me is going to be changed so that I am going to be another fellow and not myself, then you will miss it. If that is the kind of marks you are looking for, you will not find them. But if you are expecting to observe a man's flesh and blood and bones and spirit and mind indwelt by God, then you will find them—not a machine, not an automaton, or an imitation, but a clear mind and a pure heart, a son of God in nature and essence."

What is all God's effort with the world but to bring out the real man in the image of Christ—the real man with the knowledge of God? That real man, reconstructed until his very substance is the substance of God! And when you stop to reason that to its proper conclusion, it is the only way in which Jesus Christ Himself or God, the Eternal Father, will ever keep from living in loneliness forever.

When one stops to analyze that fact, we see that God is trying to make us in all our nature and being and habits and thought, in all the structure of our life, just as beautiful and just as real and just as clear-minded and just as strong as Jesus Himself. Then we understand what Christ's redemption means. It is the bringing out of Christ in you, until Christ in you is the one manifest—manifest through your eyes, just as God was manifest through the eyes of Jesus; manifest through your touch, just as God was manifest through Jesus. It is not a power or a life separate from yourself but two lives made one, two natures conjoined, two minds operating in one—Christ in you.

One day at the Chicago conference, I sat with an old colored lady one afternoon after the meeting, and she told me of her sicknesses and woes—and they were many. After a time, when she had grown somewhat still, I said, "Dear mother, how long have you been a Christian?"

She replied, "Since I was a child." Then I tried to show her that God expected a development of God and His nature and the working and action of God in her in transforming power, through the agency of the Spirit, and that there was a process of remaking and remolding that should change her nature and life and dissolve the rheumatism and Bright's disease and all the other difficulties, just as truly as long ago sin had disappeared from her soul.

After the conversation had gone on to the proper point, I said, "Dear sister, anybody can see that Christ dwells in your spirit." Her eyes were lovely, delightful! "Let your mind extend just a little. Let your thought comprehend that just as Jesus dwells in your spirit and also possesses your soul, in just exactly the same way He is possessing your blood and your kidneys and your old rheumatic bones, and that the very same thing will happen in your bones when you realize that truth as happened when you were converted at the altar."

She had told me how she had prayed twenty-two days and nights until Christ was revealed in her soul as Savior. She seemed to want to wait twenty-two days and nights for God to manifest Himself in the rheumatic bones, and I was trying to get her away from it.

She said, "Brother, lay your hands on me and pray for me, and I will be healed."

I answered, "No, I want you to get well by realizing that right now, that same Christ that dwells in your spirit and your soul is in your bones and in your blood and in your brain." Presently, the old lady hopped to her feet and said, "My God, He is." She made it. Christ had been imprisoned in her soul and spirit. Now He was permitted to manifest Himself in her body.

Brother William Seymour and the Azusa Street Revivals

Brother Tom Hezmalhalch came into a Negro meeting in Los Angeles one day where they were talking about the baptism of the Holy Ghost. He had picked up a paper and read of these peculiar meetings, among other things, that they spoke in tongues. That was new to him. He said, "If they do, and if it is real, that is an advance in the Spirit of God beyond what is common. I am going to get it."

He went and listened as the old Negro taught. He was trying to develop the thought of conscious cleansing, and he used the beautiful text: *"Now ye are clean through the word which I have spoken unto you"* (John 15:3). That became very real to Tom, and, after a while, they were invited to come and kneel at the altar to seek God for the baptism of the Holy Spirit. Tom said to me, "John, I got up and walked toward that old bench with the realization in my soul of the truth of the Word and that the real cleansing and Cleanser was in my heart."

He knelt down and prayed for a minute or two. His soul rose, and his heart believed for the baptism of the Holy Ghost. Then, he arose and took one of the front seats. One of the workers said, "Brother, don't stop praying until you are baptized in the Holy Ghost."

He replied, "Jesus told me I was baptized in the Holy Ghost."

Mr. Seymour said, "Just leave him alone. He has got it. You wait and see." A few days passed, and one day Tom said that the Spirit began to surge through him and a song of praise in tongues, angelic voice, broke through his lips.

An old preacher came into my office in Africa and said, "Brother Lake, there is something I want to talk to you about. There used to be a very remarkable manifestation in my life. It was the manifestation of tongues and interpretation. But I have not spoken in tongues for a year. I wish you would pray for me."

I said, "No, go over and lie down and get still and let God move in your life." I was writing a letter. I went on with my writing. Presently, I observed that something wanted to speak in me, and I turned my head just a little to see that the old man was speaking in tongues, and I was getting the interpretation of it as I wrote the letter.

Don't you know Christians are stumbling every day over that fact? You are doubting and fearing and wondering if Christ is there. Beloved brother and sister, give Him a chance to reveal Himself. He is there. Probably because of your lack of realization, your soul is closed, and He is not able to reveal Himself. You know God is never able in many to reveal Himself outside of the spirit or soul. The real secret of the ministry of healing is in permitting the grace of God in your heart to flow out through your hands and your nerves into the other life. That is the real secret.

And one of the greatest works God has to perform is to subject our flesh to God. Many Christians, the deepest Christians, who really know God in their spirits and enjoy communion with God, are compelled to wait until there is a process of spiritualization that takes place in their bodies before God can reveal Himself through them. Do not imprison Christ in you. Let Him live, let Him manifest, let Him find vent through you.

There is one great thing that the world is needing more than anything else, and I am convinced of it more every day I live. Mankind has one supreme need, and that is the love of God. The hearts of men are dying for lack of the love of God. I have a sister in Detroit. She came over to Milwaukee to visit us for two or three days at the convention there. As I watched her moving around, I said, "I would like to take her along and just have her love folks." She would not need to preach. You do not need to preach to folks. It is not the words you say that are going to bless them. They are in need of something greater. It is the thing in your soul. They have got to receive it, and then their soul will open and there will be a divine response. Give it to them. It is the love of Christ.

You have seen people who loved someone who would not respond. If there is any hard situation in God's earth, that is it, to really, passionately love someone and find no response in him.

I had an English friend and was present at his marriage. Some years later, he and his wife came to visit at our home. He was that cold type of closed Englishman, and she was the warm type. One day, as they started out for a walk, I noticed the passionate yearning in her soul. If he would just say something that was tender, something that would gratify the craving of her nature for affection! But he seemed to go along absolutely unconscious of it. After the lady had gone into the house, I said, "Hibbs, you are a stiff. How is it possible that you can walk down the street with a woman like your wife and not realize that her heart is craving and crying for you to turn around and say something that shows you love her?"

He said, "Do you think that is the difficulty? I will go and do it now." And everything subsided while he proceeded to do it.

What is it men are seeking? What is it their hearts are asking for when they are seeking God? What is their soul crying for? Mankind is separated from God. It may not be mountains of sin between you and God at all. It may be only that your nature is closed and unresponsive. My, when the real love touch of God is breathed into your soul, what a transformation takes place! There is probably no more delightful thing on earth than to watch a soul crying unto God when the light of God comes in and the life of God fills the nature and that holy affection that we seek from others finds expression in Him.

> When the real love touch of God is breathed into your soul, what a transformation takes place!

That is what the Lord is asking from you, and if you want to gratify the heart of Jesus Christ, that is the only way in all the world to do it. You know the invitation is not, "Give Me thine head." The invitation is, "My son, give Me thine heart." That is an affectionate relationship, a real love union in God, a real love union with God. Think of the fineness of God's purpose! He expects that same marvelous spiritual union that is brought to pass between your soul and His own to be extended, so that you embrace in that union every other soul around you.

Oh, that is what it means when it talks about being baptized in one Spirit, submerged, buried, enveloped, and enveloping in the one Spirit of God.

While I was in Milwaukee recently, I went out one morning with Rev. Fockler to make a call on a sick person. We stepped into one of the most distracted homes I have ever been in. A strange condition had developed in one of the daughters, and the household was distressed. They were the saddest group. They were German people. Fockler speaks

German. Presently, he began to talk to the household. I just sat back and watched. Presently, I noticed the faces began to relax and the strain was gone. The girl who was apparently insane came down the stairs and stood outside the door where she could not be seen except by me. He continued to converse with the family, and as their souls softened and their faith lifted, her eyes commenced to change.

She was moved upon by the same Spirit until her nature responded, too, and in just a little while she stepped into the room. She had tormented that household. Nobody could get near her. She slipped up behind Fockler's chair and stood with her hands at the back of the chair. He understood and disregarded her. After a while, she rested one hand on his shoulder. After a little while, she put the other hand on the other shoulder. And in fifteen or twenty minutes, we left that home, and there was just as much distinction between the attitudes of these dear souls when we came in and when we went out as between heaven and hell. If hell has a characteristic, it is that of distraction. If heaven has a particular characteristic, it is the presence of God, the calm of God, the power of God, the love of God.

There were days when the church could club men into obedience by preaching hell to them, but that day has long since passed. The world has outgrown it. Men are discovering there is only one way, and that is the Jesus way. Jesus did not come with a club, but with the great, loving heart of God. He was *"moved with compassion"* (Matthew 9:36; 14:14; Mark 1:41; 6:34).

This morning I lay in bed and wrote a letter, an imaginary letter, to a certain individual. I was getting ready so that when I came down, I could dictate the sentences that would carve him right. One of the phrases was, "You great big calf, come out of it and be a man." As I lay there, I got to thinking, *If Jesus was writing this letter, I wonder what He would write?* But somehow it would not frame. My soul was not in an attitude to produce such a letter. So I came down this morning and called Edna and commenced to dictate, and I was trying to dictate a letter in the Spirit of Jesus. Presently, I woke up to the fact that I was putting the crimp into it like a lawyer.

After she had it written and laid down for my signature, I commenced to read it over. It was not what I wanted to write at all. The first two paragraphs had a touch of the right spirit, but that was all. So, I laid it aside. Then I went in and prayed a little while, and after I had been praying for twenty minutes, the telephone rang, and it was that fellow.

He wanted me to come down to the Davenport Hotel, and we had three of the best hours without being aware of the time.

We boast of our development in God; we speak glowingly of our spiritual experiences, but it is only once in a while that we find ourselves in the real love of God. The greater part of the time we are in ourselves rather than in Him. This evidences just one thing—that Christ has not yet secured that perfect control of our life, that subjection of our nature, that absorption of our individuality, so that He is able to impregnate it and maintain it in Himself. We recede, we draw back, we close up. We imprison our Lord.

Beloved, the secret of a religious meeting is that it assists men's hearts to open, they become receptive, and the love of God finds vent in their nature for a little while, and they go away saying, "Didn't we have a good time? Wasn't that a splendid meeting?"

I wonder if there is anything that could not be accomplished through the love of God. Paul says there is not. Love never fails. (See 1 Corinthians 13:8.) That is one infallible state. Try it on your wife; try it on your children; try it on your neighbors.

Ah, sometimes we need to get things over on the bigger love, the greater heart. It is a good thing to detach your soul. Do not hold people. Do not bind people. Just cut them loose and let God have them. Don't you know that we hold people with such a grip when we pray for them that they miss the blessing? Why, you have such a grip that your humanity is exercising itself and the Spirit is being submerged. Let your soul relax and let the Spirit of God in you find vent. There is no substitute for the love of God. "*Christ in you.*" Oh, you have the capacity to love. All the action of the Spirit of God has its secret there.

I stood on one occasion by a dying woman who was suffering and writhing in awful agony. I had prayed again and again with no results. But, this day, something just happened inside of me. My soul broke clear down, and I saw that poor soul in a new light, and, before I knew it, I reached out and gathered her in my arms and hugged her up to my soul, not my bosom. In a minute, the real thing had taken place, and I laid her back on the pillow; in five minutes she was well. God was waiting on me, until He could give to my soul the sense of that tenderness that was in the Son of God.

> The life of God, the Spirit of God, the nature of God are sufficient for every need of man.

That is the real reason that His name is written in imperishable memory, and the name of Jesus Christ is the most revered name in earth or sea or sky. And I am eager to get that category of folks who can manifest the real love of God all the time.

The life of God, the Spirit of God, the nature of God are sufficient for every need of man. In the highest sense of the word, he is a real Christian whose body, soul, and spirit alike are filled with the life of God.

Healing in any department of the nature, whether spirit, soul, or body, is but a means to an end. The object of healing is health—abiding health—of body, soul, and spirit. The healing of the spirit unites the spirit of man to God forever. The healing of the soul corrects psychic disorder and brings the soul processes into harmony with the mind of God. And healing of the body completes the union of man with God when the Holy Spirit possesses all.

13

SPIRITUAL DOMINION

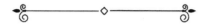

December 9, 1924

The lesson that God seems to have put in my soul tonight is found in the first chapter of 2 Timothy. Do you know that we do not read the Scriptures like people read a textbook? Have you ever observed how a scientist reads his textbook? He weighs every single word, and each word has a peculiar meaning. If we read the Word of God like that, we would get the real vitality of what it says. I wonder if we have caught the force of this Scripture:

> *Paul, an apostle of Jesus Christ by the will of God, according to the promise of* **life** *which is* **in** *Christ Jesus.* (2 Timothy 1:1)

There is no life outside of Jesus Christ—no eternal life outside of Jesus Christ, by the declaration of Jesus Himself. John said,

> *God hath given to us eternal life, and this life is in his Son. He that hath the Son hath life; and he that hath not the Son of God hath not life.* (1 John 5:11–12)

All the Scriptures are dear to my heart and bring their peculiar ministry and lesson, but the words of Jesus are the supreme words of the gospel. Jesus said:

> It is the spirit that quickeneth;...the words that I speak unto you, they **are** spirit, and they are life. (John 6:63)

Do you know, the difficulty in our day is that we have run away from Jesus? That is, the church at large has. The world is making a great struggle at the present hour—we are in the midst of it ourselves—to get *back* to Jesus. We have run into false theology, we have run into churchianity[8] and human interpretations and a hundred other follies, but, friends, it is a perfectly lovely and refreshing thing to get back to Jesus. Take the words of Jesus and let them become the supreme court of the gospel to you.

I consider all the Word of God the common court of the gospel, but the words of Jesus are the supreme court of the gospel. If there is a question that is not clearly decided according to your vision in the common court of the gospel, then refer it to the supreme court, which is the words of Jesus, and the words of Jesus will settle anything that is in your mind.

If our questions were settled by the words of Jesus, we would be out of all the confusion that the world is in at present. I do not see any other way for the world to come out of their present confusion, unless it is to accept the words of Jesus as final authority, to accept Jesus as the divine finality, where all questions are finally adjudicated, and to stay by the words of Jesus.

Just as an example on that line, I suppose there is not any question in the Scriptures that is more muddled and fuddled and slobbered over than the subject of water baptism, and we have a dozen forms of baptismal practice, emphasizing different phases of baptismal consecration. But, beloved, the Word of Jesus would settle the whole controversy. Jesus's words settle both the spirit and the mode of baptism forever. All

---

8. This is apparently Lake's own euphemism for religious Christianity.

the conflagration that the Christian world has been in over that question is because we simply refused to take the words of Jesus and believe and obey them. I am such an enthusiast on the words of Jesus that if I were compelled to choose between the practice of the apostles and the words of Jesus, I would stand by the words of Jesus. It is the only method that has kept my soul from the confusion I see in other lives.

> I am such an enthusiast on the words of Jesus that if I were compelled to choose between the practice of the apostles and the words of Jesus, I would stand by the words of Jesus.

Coming back to our lesson, observe these words:

According to the promise of life....   (2 Timothy 1:1)

There is no promise of life outside of Jesus Christ. Jesus was the most emphatic teacher the world ever saw. He said,

Ye must be born again.   (John 3:7)

And there is no arbitration by which you can get around the matter. There is no possibility of avoiding that truth. You have got to come straight to it and meet it.

According to the promise of life which is in Christ Jesus.
                    (2 Timothy 1:1)

When I call to remembrance the unfeigned faith that is in thee, which dwelt first in thy grandmother Lois, and thy mother Eunice; and I am persuaded that in thee also.   (verse 5)

Timothy had two generations behind him of women of faith.

*Wherefore I put thee in remembrance that thou stir up the gift of God, which is in thee **by the putting on of my hands**.*

(2 Timothy 1:6)

Paul had some faith in the value of the putting on of his hands. It was not a mere form. I want to call your attention to the Word of God especially on this line. Paul's own convictions were that through the laying on of hands on this young man, an impartation of God to his life had been given. It was so real that even though Timothy was not aware of it and was not exercising the power of God thus bestowed, yet Paul's conviction was that the power of God was present. Why? Because he had laid his hands on him in the name of the Lord Jesus Christ, and he believed the Spirit of the Lord Jesus Christ had been imparted to him; therefore, the gift of God was in him. Therefore, the faith to exercise that gift ought to be present and be believed it was present because of the fact that the faith of God had already dwelt in his mother and grandmother, and he believed in him also.

Beloved, it takes faith to exercise your gift of God. There are just lots of people around everywhere who have gifts of God, and they are lying dormant in their lives, and there is no value for the kingdom of God through them because of the fact that they have no faith in God to put the gift in exercise and get the benefit of it.

Probably Timothy was a timid fellow, and Paul is going to show him why he should be exercising this gift of God which he believed to be in him.

For God hath not given us the spirit of fear.   (2 Timothy 1:7)

I confess I would like to swear sometimes, and I would like to say, "To h— with preachers who are all the time preaching fear." They preach fear of the devil and fear of demons and fear of this influence and fear of that influence and fear of some other power. If the Holy Ghost has come from heaven into your soul, common sense teaches us that He has made you the master thereby of every other power in the world. Otherwise, the Word of God is a blank falsehood, for it declares,

> *Greater is he that is in you, than he that is in the world.*
>
> (1 John 4:4)

> *Behold, I give unto you power to tread on serpents and scorpions, and over all the power of the enemy: and nothing shall by any means hurt you.* (Luke 10:19)

And if we had faith to believe that the *"greater than he"* is in us, bless God, we would be stepping out with boldness and majesty. The conscious supremacy of the Son of God would be manifest in our lives, and instead of our being subservient and bowed down and broken beneath the weight of sin and the powers of darkness around us, they would flee from us and keep out of our way. I believe before God there is not a devil comes within a hundred feet of a real, God-anointed Christian. That is the kind of vision God put in my soul.

When I went to South Africa years ago, I attended a great missionary conference a short time after I was there. It was a general conference of the Christian missions of the country. On account of our teaching the baptism of the Holy Ghost and the power of God to heal, we were a peculiar feature in the conference. We were bringing a new message, and they wanted to hear us and get us sized up and classified.

Among the difficulties they discussed in that conference was the tremendous influence of the native medicine men over the people. They call them witch doctors. They are a powerfully developed, psychic-type of man, and for generations and generations they have studied psychic things until they understand the practice of psychic laws. It is marvelous to see the psychic manifestations they bring to pass. I have seen shocking things take place at the hand of witch doctors, things that nobody would believe unless you beheld them.

On one occasion, two men had become extremely jealous of each other, both native chiefs, and they lived sixty miles from each other. One time, as I was in the kraal[9] of one of them, I heard them discussing this difficulty with the other chief, and it was decided by the chief that the next Sunday morning he was going to set the other fellow on fire. I wanted to see this phenomenon, and I got a horse and went across the country to be there on Sunday morning.

The chiefs go out and round up their cattle and herds, look over their flocks, etc. It is a sort of Sunday exercise. I rode along. We had not ridden for more than an hour when I observed this fellow was becoming very hot. Within half an hour, he was absolutely purple. I knew somewhat of medicine; I would have said the man was likely to have a paralytic stroke from blood pressure. After a while, he began to complain of terrible pain, and finally he became exhausted, got down and lay on the ground, and passed into a state of terrible exhaustion. I believe the man would have died. I had heard about these sorts of things, but this was taking place under my own eyes. I saw that unless the man got deliverance, he would die. When it got to that point, I said to the brethren, "It is time that we prayed." I stepped over and laid my hands on and called on God to destroy that damning psychic power that was destroying the fellow, and God shattered it.

I talked to the conference about this matter. I said, "It is a strange thing to me that in all the years of missions in this land, your hands are tied on account of witch doctors. Why don't you go out and cast the devil out of these fellows and get the people delivered from their power?"

They took a long breath and said, "Cast the devil out? He will cast the devil out of you!" The secret of our work, the reason God gave us one hundred thousand people, the reason we have twelve hundred native preachers in our work in Africa, is because of the fact we believed the promise of:

Greater is he that is in you, than he that is in the world.

(1 John 4:4)

---

9. *kraal*: a village of South African natives.

We not only went to seek them, but challenged them separately and unitedly and, by the power of God, delivered the people from their power, and when they were delivered, the people appreciated their deliverance from the slavery in which they had been held through their superstitious, psychological spirit control, and they are most terrible.

God hath not given us the spirit of fear; but of power, and of love, and of a sound mind. (2 Timothy 1:7)

Whenever I got in the presence of one of these fellows and wanted to cast out the devil, I always felt I wanted to get his eye. I search to get his eye. The eyes of a man are the windows of his soul. In teaching a class of children, I asked them what the eyes were for. One little chap said, "Your eyes are for you to look out of." Do you get it? It is not a poetic expression; they are the windows through which you look out. It is wonderful, the things you see when you look out. Sometimes you see fear and the spirit of darkness, and you see the devil in the other life. Marvelous things that you see with your inner eyes.

The world laughs at our Pentecostal people because they sometimes talk about seeing by the Spirit, and sometimes we talk about seeing psychically. We see all the time naturally, as you and I do now.

God anoints your soul. God anoints your life. God comes to dwell in your person. God comes to make you a master. That is the purpose of His indwelling in a Christian. The real child of God was to be a master over every other power of darkness in the world. (See Luke 9:1; 10:19.) It was to be subject to him. He is to be God's representative in the world. (See Ephesians 6:11–12; 2 Corinthians 5:20.) The Holy Ghost in the Christian was to be as powerful as the Holy Ghost was in the Christ. Indeed, Jesus's words go to such an extreme that they declare that:

Greater works than these shall he do. (John 14:12)

It indicates that the mighty Holy Ghost from heaven in the life of the Christian was to be more powerful in you and in me after Jesus got to heaven and ministered Him to our souls than He was in Jesus.

Beloved, who has the faith to believe it? Who has faith to exercise it? We cannot exercise anything beyond what we believe to be possible. Listen:

> *God hath not given us the spirit of fear.* (2 Timothy 1:7)

Fear of the devil is nonsense. Fear of demons is foolish. The Spirit of God anointing the Christian heart makes the soul impregnable to the powers of darkness. How I love to teach men that when the Lord Jesus Christ anoints your soul and baptizes you in the Holy Ghost, the almightiness of the eternal God the Father, by the Spirit and Jesus Christ combined, has come into your soul.

One of the thirty-six articles of the Church of England says, "The Holy Ghost which proceedeth from the Father and the Son." There is no truer thing in all the world. Do you get it—"which proceedeth from the Father and the Son"? In the fourth and fifth chapters of Revelation, you see the distinctive personalities of God the Father and Jesus Christ. God the Father occupies the throne and is holding the seven-sealed book in His hand. And Jesus Christ, the silent Lamb, without an attendant, not an angel to accompany Him, absolutely alone, in lonesomeness as the slain Lamb, presents Himself to the Father, and the Father hands Him the seven-sealed book as He whose right it is to unseal and open the seals.

What I want to bring to you is that the Spirit of God, the divine master, the eternal power of God, the combined life and presence by the Spirit, of the Father and the Son, is given to you—not to leave you a weakling and subject to all kinds of powers of darkness, but to make you a master, to give you dominion in God over every devilish force that ever was.

God hath not given us the spirit of fear; but of power, and of love,
and of a sound mind. (2 Timothy 1:7)

The Spirit of power is the Holy Ghost, bless God. And not only of power, but of love and of a sound mind—not craziness and insanity, but a sound mind, by which you can look in the face of the devil and laugh.

The Spirit of power is the Holy Ghost. And not only of power, but of love and of a sound mind.

Once I was called to come to pray for a blacksmith at Johannesburg, South Africa. He was in delirium tremens.[10] When I got to the house, they had him locked in a room and the windows barred. The wife said, "Mr. Lake, you are not going into that room?"

I said, "Yes, I would like to."

"But, brother, you do not understand. My sons are all more powerful than you are, and four of them tried to overpower him and could not do it. He nearly killed them."

I said, "Dear sister, I have the secret of power that I believe matches this case."

Greater is he that is in you, than he that is in the world.
(1 John 4:4)

"Sister, you just give me the key, and go about your work, and do not be troubled." I unlocked the door, slipped into the room, turned the key again, and put the key in my pocket. The man was reclining in a crouch like a lion ready to spring. I never heard any lips blaspheme as his did. He cursed maybe every expression I ever heard and worse. He threatened me that if I came near him, he would tear me limb from limb

10. *delirium tremens*: a violent restlessness due to excessive use of alcohol, characterized by trembling.

and throw me out the window. He was as big as two of me. I never saw such an arm in my life.

I began to talk to him. I had the confidence that *"greater is he that is in you, than he that is in the world."* I engaged him in conversation until the Holy Ghost in me got hold of that devil, or a legion, as the case might be. I approached the bed step-by-step, sometimes only three inches, and in half an hour I got up close enough where I could reach his hand. He was still reclining in a posture like a lion. I caught his hand and turned his wrists. I was not practicing any athletic tricks, but I unconsciously turned his wrists over, and as I did it brought my eyes down near his, and all at once I woke up. I could see the devil in that man begin to crawl. He was trying to get away. God Almighty can look out of your eyes, and every devil that was ever in hell could not look in the eyes of Jesus without crawling. The lightning bolts of God were there.

My spirit awoke, and I could see the devil was in terror and was crawling and trying to get back away from my eyes as far as he could. I looked up to heaven and called on God to cast that devil out and lent Jesus Christ all the force of my nature, all the power of my spirit, all the power of my mind, and all the power of my body. God had me from the crown of my head to the soles of my feet. The lightning bolts of God went through me, and the next thing I knew, he collapsed in a heap and flopped down like a big fish. Then he turned out of the bed on his knees and began to weep and pray, because he had become human again, and the devil was gone.

Dear hearts, don't you see in a moment that the character of education develops a certain confidence in God, and it makes your soul sick when you see Christian men and women sneak around afraid of the devil and teaching people the devil is going to jump on you and take possession of you? Not a bit of it! There never was a devil in the world that ever went through the blood of Jesus, if the individual was in Christ.

In the Jewish Bible, among the listings of the covenants is one that is known as the Threshold Covenant. That was the covenant by which the Israelites went out of the land of Egypt, when God told them to slay a lamb and put the blood on the doorposts and lintel. And the Jewish

Bible adds that they put the blood on the threshold. A lot of people get the blood of Jesus on their head, but it seems to me they do not get it under their feet. The Word of God teaches us to get the blood under our feet and on the right hand and on the left hand and over our head. That is our protection. There was no angel of death in the land of Egypt, or in hell, that could go through that blood unto that family. No sir! He was absolutely barred.

Friends, do you believe it was the blood of the Lamb that was barring the angel of death? Do you believe the red stains on the doors frightened him away? No, sir. The blood signified to me that there is one that goes *through* the blood, and that is the Holy Ghost. And, beloved, the eternal God, by the Spirit, went through the blood to the inside and stayed there and defended the house.

Greater is he that is in you, than he that is in the world.

(1 John 4:4)

All these little insignificant devils that come along in this sickness or that sickness or that temptation of sin have no power over you. Dear friends, from heaven there comes to your heart and mine that dominion of Jesus by which the God-anointed soul walks through them, through myriads of demons, and they cannot touch you.

I was in Pretoria, South Africa, visiting with a friend and trying to keep out of the hot sun to meditate and pray; and as I meditated and prayed, I seemed to be lifted up in the Spirit until I was a mile or more above the city and could see the city like you would from an airplane. When I got up there, I made a discovery. There were myriads of spirits of darkness and myriads of spirits of light in the most awful conflict I ever saw. Naturally, you think of a weapon when you see a fight. I thought, *If only I had a weapon, I would get into that fight.*

Presently, the Spirit of God got hold of me, and when these demons came at me from all sides, I waded into them and began to knock them down. It continued until I had knocked so many down I had to climb over them to get at the rest.

When the vision lifted, I prayed, "Dear Lord, what does it mean?" And the Spirit of the Lord said to me, "This contest that you have seen in the upper air will exist among your own people on the earth in six months. This lesson is to teach you that there is a dominion in Jesus Christ, and *'greater is he that is in you, than he that is in the world.'*"

Friends, it is time you and I, as the blood-washed in Jesus, awoke to our privilege whereby in the name of the Lord we cease to sin and let no unholy condemnation remain upon our life any longer.

I do not know, but maybe I have come through a different school from what others have in the lines of the Spirit, but I am sure of one thing: that if Christianity was to leave me a weakling to be oppressed by the power of darkness, I would seek something else because it would not meet the need. It is that which meets the need that gives you divine supremacy in Jesus Christ. Friends, when your heart is surcharged by that faith in God so that *"greater is he that is in you, than he that is in the world,"* you will pray a new prayer.

Moses came to the Red Sea with impassable mountains on the right hand and impassable mountains on the left hand, the army of Pharaoh behind him, and the sea in front of him. If any man had a right to stop and pray, surely you might say that man had.

Over and over and over again, when we get to the real ditch, we try to jump the thing and put the responsibility back on God. Just watch God make a real man. When Moses got his prayer nicely started, God rebuked him and said,

> *Wherefore criest thou unto me? speak, unto the children of Israel, that they go forward: but lift* **thou** *up thy rod, and stretch out* **thine** *hand over the sea, and* **divide** *it.* (Exodus 14:15–16)

I want you Pentecostal Christians to get this. God did not say, "Moses, you stretch forth your hand, and I will divide the sea." He said, "Stretch forth *thine* hand over the sea, and *divide* it. You have faith in

Me; you stretch forth your hand and divide the sea." Jesus said practically the same thing to His disciples:

When he had called unto him his twelve disciples, he gave them power against unclean spirits, to cast them out, and to heal all manner of sickness and all manner of disease.
(Matthew 10:1; see also Luke 9:1–6)

Beloved, He gives it to you. What is the Holy Ghost? It is the gift of God Himself to you. The Holy Spirit is not simply given that you may be a channel and always a channel. No, sir! But, instead of that, the most magnificent thing the Word of God portrays is that Christ indwelling in you by the Holy Ghost is to make you a son of God like Jesus Christ, God-anointed from heaven, with the recognized power of God in your spirit to command the will of God.

It may not be that all souls have grown to that place where such a life as that is evident, but surely, if the Son of God by the Holy Ghost has been born in our hearts, it is time we began to let Him have some degree of sway in our hearts, and some degree of heavenly dominion of value, and some degree of the lightning bolts of Jesus Christ breaking forth from our spirits.

That is what the Word of God speaks to my soul tonight. That is why my spirit rejoices in this blessed Word.

God hath not given us the spirit of fear; but of power, and of love, and of a sound mind.   (2 Timothy 1:7)

The sanest man is the man who believes God and stands on His promises and knows the secret of His power and receives the Holy Ghost and gives Him sway in his life and goes out in the name of the Lord Jesus to command the will of God and bring it to pass in the world.

At the end of the first three hundred years of the Christian era, there were millions of Christians. Christianity was an aggressive power. Christianity went into the heart of heathendom to undo their superstitions, to break down their psychological forces, to leave the consciousness of Jesus Christ in the heart, to heal the sick, to raise the dead. O, God in heaven, bring our hearts back to it. Christianity was a conquering force.

But friends, there was a consecration secret in the life of the early church. It was this: If they could not conquer, they could die. Dear friends, you will never exercise very much of the dominion of the Son of God in your spirit until your heart is ready to say, "If I cannot get the mastery, I can die." The early Christians died, plenty of them—millions of them. That is the reason people say the blood of the martyrs was the seed of the church. Bless God, they died for their faith.

Friends, you and I will never know or have the big ministry and the big victory until our souls have arrived at the place where we will die for our faith also. Lord God, help us. These days, if a man gets a stomachache, he is afraid he will die. Die if you have to die, but do not disgrace the cause of Christ and weaken in your faith and sell it to man or the devil. When that degree of consecration comes into your heart, when that degree of determination comes into your spirit, you will not have to die.

But I tell you, most of us will do our dying before we enter there. That is the life into which dead men enter. That is the resurrection life. We have to die to get it. You have to die to enter there. We die to our sin, we die to ourselves, we die to the opinions of men, and we die to the old world. We die to fear of spooks and demons and devils and prove the truth of the text, "*Greater is he that is in you, than he that is in the world*" (1 John 4:4). "*In my name shall they cast out devils*" (Mark 16:17). "*Resist the devil, and he will flee from you*" (James 4:7). We live in Jesus Christ. Blessed be His name.

Neither give place to the devil. (Ephesians 4:27)

Put on the whole armour of God, that ye may be able to stand against the wiles of the devil. (Ephesians 6:11)

There hath no temptation taken you but such as is common to man: but God is faithful, who will not suffer you to be tempted above that ye are able; but will with the temptation also make a way to escape, that ye may be able to bear it.   (1 Corinthians 10:13)

And Jesus said unto them, Because of your unbelief: for verily I say unto you, If ye have faith as a grain of mustard seed, ye shall say unto this mountain, Remove hence to yonder place; and it shall remove; and nothing shall be impossible unto you.   (Matthew 17:20)

Behold, I give unto you power to tread on serpents and scorpions, and over all the power of the enemy: and nothing shall by any means hurt you.   (Luke 10:19)

14

SPIRITUAL HUNGER

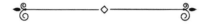

December 11, 1924
Portland, Oregon

The Scripture text tonight is: *"Blessed are they which do hunger and thirst after righteousness: for they shall be filled"* (Matthew 5:6).

Hunger is a mighty good thing. It is the greatest persuader I know of. It is a marvelous mover. Nations have learned that you can do most anything with people until they get hungry. But when they get hungry, you want to watch out. There is a certain spirit of desperation that accompanies hunger.

I wish we all had it spiritually. I wish to God we were desperately hungry. Wouldn't it be glorious? Somebody would get filled before this meeting is over. It would be a strange thing if we were all desperately hungry for God for only one or two to get filled in a service.

"Blessed are they which do hunger and thirst after righteousness." Righteousness is just the rightness of God—the rightness of God in your spirit; the rightness of God in your soul; the rightness of God in your body; the rightness of God in your affairs, in your home, in your business, everywhere.

God is an all-round God. His power operates from every side. The artists put a halo around the head of Jesus to show that there is a radiation of glory in His person. They might just as well put it around His feet or any part of His person. It is the radiant glory of the indwelling God, radiating out through the personality. There is nothing more wonderful than the indwelling of God in the human life. The most supreme marvel that God ever performed was when He took possession of those who are hungry.

"Blessed are they which do hunger." I will guarantee to you that after the crucifixion of Jesus, there were a hundred and twenty mighty hungry folks at Jerusalem. I do not believe if they had not been mightily hungry they would have gotten so gloriously filled. It was because they were hungry that they were filled.

We are sometimes inclined to think of God as mechanical, as though God set a date for this event or that to occur. But my opinion is that one of the works of the Holy Ghost is that of preparer. He comes and prepares the heart of men in advance by putting a strange hunger for that event that has been promised by God until it comes to pass.

The more I study history and prophecy, the more I am convinced that when Jesus was born into the world, He was born in answer to a tremendous heart cry on the part of the world. The world needed God desperately. They wanted a manifestation of God tremendously, and Jesus Christ as the Deliver and Savior came in answer to their soul cry.

Many look forward to the second coming of Jesus—His coming again—as though mechanically, on a certain date, when certain events come to pass, Jesus is going to arrive. I do not see it that way. I see on the other hand that there must be a tremendous hunger, an overwhelming hunger, for the Lord's coming in the hearts of men, so that a prayer such as was never prayed in the world before for Christ to come will rise to heaven. And, bless God, when it rises to heaven on the part of sufficient souls, it will take Jesus Christ Himself off the throne and bring Him down to earth.

Daniel says that he was convinced by the study of the books of prophecy, especially that of Jeremiah, that the time had come when they ought to be delivered from captivity in Babylon. The seventy years was fulfilled, but there was no deliverance. So he diligently set his face to pray it into being. (See Daniel 9.)

Here is what I want you to get. If it was going to come to pass mechanically, by a certain date, there would not have been any necessity for Daniel to get that hunger in his soul, so that he fasted and prayed in sackcloth and ashes that deliverance might come.

No sir, God's purposes come to pass when your heart and mine get the real God cry, and the real God prayer comes into our spirit, and the real God yearning gets our nature. Something is going to happen then.

No difference what it may be your soul is covering or desiring, if it becomes in your life the supreme cry—not the secondary matter, or the third, or the fourth, or fifth or tenth, but the *first* thing, the supreme desire of your soul, the paramount issue—all the powers and energies of your spirit, of your soul, and of your body are reaching out and crying to God for the answer. It is going to come, it is going to come, it is going to come.

I lived in a family where for thirty-two years they never were without an invalid in the home. Before I was twenty-four years of age, we had buried four brothers and four sisters, and four other members of the family were dying, hopeless and helpless invalids. I set up my own home and married a beautiful woman. Our first son arrived. It was only a short time until I saw that same devilish train of sickness that followed Father's family had come into mine. My wife became an invalid; my son was a sickly child.

Out of it all, one thing developed in my nature—a cry for deliverance. I did not know any more about the subject of healing than an Indian, notwithstanding I was a Methodist evangelist. But my heart was crying for deliverance; my soul had come to the place where I had vomited up dependence on man. My father spent a fortune on the family, to no avail, as if there was no stoppage to the hell. And, let me tell you, there is no *human stoppage* because the thing settled deep in the nature of man—too deep for any material remedy to get at it. It takes the almighty God and the Holy Spirit and the Lord Jesus Christ to get down into the depth of man's nature and find the real difficulty that is there and destroy it.

My brother, I want to tell you, if you are a sinner tonight and away from God, your heart is longing and your spirit asking and your soul crying for God's deliverance. He will be on hand to deliver. You will not have to cry very long until you see that the mountains are being moved, and the angel of deliverance will be there.

I finally got to that place where my supreme cry was for deliverance. Tears were shed for deliverance for three years before the healing of God came to us. I could hear the groans and cries and sobs and feel the wretchedness of our family's soul. My heart cried, my soul sobbed, my spirit wept tears. I did not know enough to call directly on God for it. Isn't it a strange thing that men do not have sense enough to have faith in God for all their needs; do not know enough to call directly on God for physical difficulties, as well as spiritual ones? But I did not.

But, bless God, one thing matured in my heart—a real hunger. And the hunger of a man's soul must be satisfied. It must be satisfied. It is a law of God; that law of God is in the depth of the Spirit. God will answer the heart that cries. God will answer the soul that asks. Christ Jesus comes to us with divine assurance and invites us when we are hungry to pray, to *believe*, to take from the Lord that which our soul covets and our heart asks for.

So, one day, the Lord of heaven came our way, and in a little while the cloud of darkness, that midnight of hell, that curse of death, was lifted and the light of God shone into our life and into our home, just the same as it existed in other men's lives and other men's homes. We learned the truth of Jesus and were able to apply the divine power of God. We were healed of the Lord.

"Blessed are they which do hunger." Friends, begin to pray to get hungry.

At this point I want to tell you a story. I was out on a snowshoe trip at St. Marie, Michigan, where they used to have four and five feet of snow. I tramped for thirty miles on my snowshoes. I was tired and weary. I arrived home and found my wife had gone away to visit, so I went over to my sister's home. I found they were also out. I went into the house and began to look for something to eat. I was nearly starved. I found a great big sort of cake that looked like corn bread. It was still quite warm and it smelled good. I ate it all.

I thought it was awful funny stuff, and it seemed to have lumps in it. I did not just understand the combination, and I was not much of a cook. About the time I had finished it, my sister and her husband came in. She said, "My, you must be awful tired and hungry."

I said, "I was, but I just found a corn cake and ate the whole thing."

She said, "My goodness, John, you did not eat that?"

I said, "What was it, Irene?"

"Why, that was a kind of cow bread we grind up, cobs and all."

You see, it depends on the character and degree of your hunger. Most anything tastes mighty good to a hungry man.

Most anything tastes mighty good to a hungry man.

If you wanted to confer a peculiar blessing on men at large, it would not be to give them pie, but to make them hungry, and then everything that came their way would taste everlastingly good.

I love to tell this story because it is the story of a hungry man. A short while afterwards, I went to South Africa, and God had begun to work very marvelously in the city of Johannesburg. A butcher who lived in the suburbs was advised by his physicians that he had developed such a tubercular state that he might not live more than nine months. He wanted to make provision in order that his family would be cared for after he was gone. He bought a farm and undertook to develop it, so that when he died, his family would have a means of existence.

One day, he received a letter from friends at Johannesburg, telling of the coming of what they spoke of as "the American brethren" and of the wonderful things that were taking place. Of how So-and-so, a terrible drunkard, had been converted; of his niece, who had been an invalid in a wheelchair for five years and had been healed of God; how one of his other relatives had been baptized in the Holy Ghost with speaking in tongues; how other friends and neighbors had been baptized and healed; of the powerful change that had come in the community; and all the marvels a vigorous work for God produces.

Dan Von Vuuren took the letter and crawled under an African thorn tree. He spread the matter out before God and began to discuss it with the Lord. He said, "God in heaven, if You could come to Mr. So-and-so, a drunkard, and deliver him from his drunkenness, save his soul, and put the joy of God in him; if You could come to this niece of mine, save her soul and heal her body and send her out to be a blessing instead of a weight and burden upon her friends; if You could come to So-and-so, so he was baptized in the Holy Ghost and spoke in tongues; Lord, if You can do these things at Johannesburg, You can do something for me, too."

And he knelt down, put his face to the ground, and cried to God that God would do something for him. And don't forget it, friends—I have a conviction that that morning, Dan Von Vuuren was so stirred by the reading of that letter that his desire to be made whole got bigger than anything else in his consciousness. His heart reached for God, and, bless God, that morning, his prayer went through to heaven, and God came down into his life. In ten minutes, he took all the breath he wanted. The pain was gone. The tuberculosis disappeared. He was a whole man.

But that was not all. He not only received a great physical healing, but God had literally come in and taken possession of the man's life until he did not understand himself anymore. In telling me, he said, "Brother, a new prayer from heaven is in my spirit. I had prayed for my wife's salvation for eighteen years, but I could never pray through. But that morning I prayed through. It was all done when I got to the house. She stood and looked at me for two minutes, until it dawned in her that I was gloriously healed of God. She never asked a question as to how it took place but fell on her knees, threw her hands up to heaven, and said, 'Pray for me, Dan. For God's sake, pray for me. I must find God today,' and God came to her soul."

He had eleven children, splendid young folks. The mother and he went to praying, and inside of a week the whole household of thirteen had been baptized in the Holy Ghost. He went to his brother's farm, told the wonder of what God had done, and prayed through, and in a little while, nineteen families were baptized in the Holy Ghost.

God so filled his life with His glory that one morning, God said to him, "Go to Pretoria. I am going to send you to the different members of Parliament." He was admitted into the presence of Premier Louis Botha. Botha told me about it afterward. He said, "Lake, I had known Von Vuuren from the time he was a boy. I had known him as a reckless, rollicking fellow. But that man came into my office and stood ten feet from my desk. I looked up, and before he commenced to speak, I began to shake and rattle on my chair. I knelt down. I had to put my head under the desk and cry out to God. Why, he looked like God; he talked like God." He had the majesty of God; he was superhumanly wonderful.

Then, he went to the office of the Secretary of State, then to the Secretary of the Treasury. Almost the same thing took place in every instance. For eighteen days God kept him going from this one and that one—lawyers, judges, and officials in the land—until every high official

184 of the Flow of the Spirit

knew there was a God and a Christ and a Savior and a baptism of the Holy Spirit, because Dan Von Vuuren had really hungered after God.

Blessed are they which do hunger. (Matthew 5:6)

I was sitting here tonight before the meeting and began reading an old sermon I had preached to a men's club at Spokane, Washington, eight years ago, entitled "The Calling of the Soul." In it, I observed I had recounted the story of the original people who came to the Parham School in 1900 and whom, in answer to the cries of their souls, God came and baptized in the Holy Ghost. All the Apostolic Faith Churches and Missions, Assemblies of God, and other movements are the result.

I knew Brother Parham's wife and his sister-in-law, Lillian Thistleweight. She was the woman who brought the light of God for real sanctification to my heart. It was not her preaching or her words. I sat in Fred Bosworth's home one night before a night of preaching the gospel. I listened to that woman telling of the Lord and His love and sanctifying grace and power and what real holiness was. It was not arguments or logic; it was she herself. It was the divine holiness that came from her soul. It was the living Spirit of God that came out of the woman's life.

I went back in the room, as far away as I could get. I was self-satisfied, doing for the world, well in the world, prosperous with all the accompaniments that go with successful business, but that night my heart got so hungry that I fell on my knees, and those who were present will tell you yet that they had never heard anybody pray as I prayed. Bosworth said long afterward, "Lake, there is one instance that I shall always remember in your life; that was the night you prayed in my home until the rafters shook, until God came down, until the fire struck, until our souls melted, until God came and sanctified our hearts." All the devils in hell and out of hell could not believe there is not a real sanctified experience in Jesus Christ; when God comes in and makes your heart pure and takes self out of your nature and gives you divine triumph over sin and self, blessed be the name of the Lord!

Blessed are they which do hunger. (Matthew 5:6)

Beloved, pray to get hungry.

Getting back to Dan Von Vuuren. For several years before I left Africa, he went up and down the land like a burning fire. Everywhere he went, sinners were saved and were healed. Men and women were baptized in the Holy Ghost, until he set the districts on fire with the power of God; and he is going still.

Here is a point I want to bring to you. As I talked with Lillian Thistleweight, I observed the one supreme thing in that woman's soul was the consciousness of holiness. She said, "Brother, that is what we prayed for; that is what the baptism brought to us."

Later, Brother Parham was preaching in Texas. A colored man by the name of Seymour came into his meeting. In a hotel in Chicago, he related his experience to Brother Tom and myself. I want you to see the hunger in that colored man's soul. He said he was a waiter in a restaurant and also preached to a church of colored people. He knew God as Savior, as the sanctifier. He knew the power of God to heal. But as he listened to Parham, he became convinced of a bigger thing—the baptism of the Holy Ghost. He went on to Los Angeles without receiving it, but he said he was determined to preach all he knew of God to the people.

He said, "Brother, before I met Parham, such a hunger to have more of God was in my heart that I prayed for five hours a day for two-and-a-half years. I got to Los Angeles, and when I got there, the hunger was not less but more. I prayed, 'God, what can I do?' And the Spirit said, 'Pray more.'" He said, "I am praying five hours a day now. I increased my hours of prayer to seven, and I prayed on for a year-and-a-half more. I prayed God to give me what Parham preached, the real Holy Ghost and fire with tongues and love and power of God like the apostles had."

There are better things to be had in spiritual life, but they must be sought out with faith and prayer. I want to tell you, God Almighty had put the hunger into that man's heart, that when the fire of God came, it glorified. I do not believe that any other man in modern times had a more wonderful deluge of God in his life than God gave to that dear fellow. Brother Seymour preached to my congregation, to ten thousand people, when the glory and power of God were upon his preaching and when men shook and trembled and cried to God. God was in him.

Blessed are they which do hunger...for they shall be filled.
(Matthew 5:6)

I wonder what we are hungering for. Have we a real divine hunger, something our heart is asking for? If you have, God will answer. God will answer. By every law of the Spirit that men know, the answer is due to come. It will come! Bless God, it will come. It will come in more ways than you ever dreamed of. God is not given to manifesting Himself in tongues and interpretation alone. His life in man is rounded.

When I was a lad, I accompanied my father on a visit to the office of John A. McCall, the great insurance man. We were taken to McCall's office in his private elevator. It was the first time I had ever been in a great office building and ridden in an elevator, and I remember holding my breath until the thing stopped. Then, we went into this office, the most beautiful office I had ever beheld. The rugs were so thick, I was afraid I would go through the floor when I stepped on them. His desk was a marvel, pure mahogany, and on the top of his desk, inlaid in mother-of-pearl was his name, written in script. It was so magnificent that in my boyish attitude, I said, "I'm going to have an office just like this and a desk like that with my name on it when I am a man."

I did not know how much of an asking it was in my nature, and it seemed sometimes my desire had drifted away, until I was in my thirtieth year. I was invited to come to Chicago to join an association of men who were establishing a life insurance association. They said, "Lake, we want you to manage this association." We dickered about the matter for three weeks until they came to my terms, and finally the president said, "Step into this office until we show you something. We have a surprise for you." And I stepped into an office just exactly the duplicate of John McCall's office, and there in the center was a desk of pure mahogany and instead of the name of John A. McCall it was John G. Lake, in mother-of-pearl. I had never spoken of that soul desire to a person in the world.

Friends, there is something in the call of the soul that is creative. It brings things to pass. Don't you know that when the supreme desire of your heart is known to God, all the spiritual energy of your nature and the powers of God given to you begin to concentrate and work along that certain line and form, and there comes by the unconscious creative exercise of faith into being that which our soul calls for? That is the creative action of faith, you and God together, evidencing the power of creative desire.

Interpretation of a Message in Tongues

(Mrs. James Wilson—Brother Myreen)

You shall receive the desire of your heart if you come before Me in prayer and supplication, for I am a God that answers My children. Go ye forward in the battle, for I shall be with you and fulfill the desire of your heart. Yea, pray that ye may become hungry.

Call, and I shall answer, for I am a God that hears. I shall answer your call. Come before Me. Humble yourselves before My feet, and I shall answer your call.

Be diligent before Me, and pray, yea, be ye in prayer and supplication, for you are living in the last days, and My Spirit shall not always strive with men. But ye who humble yourselves before Me will know I shall be your God, I shall strengthen you on the right hand and on the left, and ye shall understand and know that I am your living God.

As Moses stood at the Red Sea, he tried to back out of that relationship God was establishing and tried to throw the responsibility back on

God. He was overwhelmed. It was too marvelous. Surely, God must not have meant it, but God knew. When he began to recognize himself as an individual and God as another, it was offensive to God. He thought he could back up and pray for God to do something for him, the same as God did in the old relationship. He could not do it. When he got down to pray, in the mind of God, the idea of Moses not backing water and getting out of that close place, that inner relationship, that divine symphony of Moses' soul and God's, it was offensive to him. And God said, "*Wherefore criest thou unto me?*" (Exodus 14:15).

In other words, "Shut up your praying. Get up out of there."

Lift thou up thy rod, and stretch out thine hand over the sea, and divide it. (Exodus 14:16)

God did not say, "Moses, you stretch forth your hand, and I will divide the sea." He said, "*Stretch out thine hand over the sea, and divide it.*"

"You and I are one; stretch forth your hand and divide the sea. You have all there is of Me, and I have all there is of you. We are one and indivisible." God and man become one. The heart of man, the mind of man, the soul of man, enters into God, and God into him. The divine fires of the eternal Christ, by the Holy Ghost, come from heaven, and the lightning bolts of Jesus flash through the life, bless God, and the powers of Christ invigorate and manifest and demonstrate through that relationship.

God revealed that to my soul in the days when I first went to Africa, within six weeks after my feet touched the soil, and before God had given me a white church to preach in. I said, "Lord, when You give me a church in which to preach this gospel, I will preach the highest and holiest thing God's Spirit reveals to my heart. I do not care if anybody else believes it or sees it; I am going to preach the vision the Son of God puts in my soul."

Bless God, He put the high vision of the glorified Christ and the glorified Christian—not a man simply saved from sin, but a man saved from his sins, sanctified by power, infilled with His Spirit, recreated with and in Jesus Christ—one in nature, character, and substance. My heart began to preach it, my mouth gave the message, my soul sent forth the word, and my spirit called such that wanted to be the character of man to come to the feet of the Son of God and receive His blessing and receive His power. And, beloved, I tell you that in all the modern world, there was another hundred and twenty-five preachers who went out of a church to proclaim the power of God with greater power than that first hundred and twenty-five preachers. The thing that was in my soul fired Dan Von Vuuren's soul and kindled the faith of the people. Wherever it spread, it set men on fire for God.

Friends, we need a coming up into God. This church, and the church around, needs to come up into God. We have been traveling around in a circle, digging our noses in the ground, and we have had our eyes on the ground instead of in the clouds, instead of up at the throne. Look up to the glorified One! I want to see His bleeding hands. Look to heaven, where He is, to see them. Do not go back to Calvary to see Him. He is the risen, regnant,[11] glorified Son of God, risen with all power and all authority, with the keys of hell and of death! He is the divine authority, the eternal overcoming, the divine manifestation of God. And you and the regnant, glorified Christ as one are the divine manifestation of God. Come up to the throne, dear ones. Let the throne life and the throne love and the throne power and the throne spirit and the Holy Ghost in heaven possess you, and you will be a new man in Christ Jesus! And your tread will be the march of the conqueror, and your song the song of victory, and your crown the crown of glory, and your power the power of God.

---

11. *regnant*: reigning in one's own right and not as a consort.

15

DEDICATION

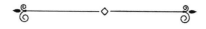

January 1925

As a basis of a little talk, I want to quote Lincoln's Gettysburg Address:

> Fourscore and seven years ago, our fathers brought forth on this continent a new nation, conceived in liberty, and dedicated to the proposition that all men are created equal. Now we are engaged in a great civil war, testing whether that nation, or any nation so conceived and so dedicated, can long endure. We are met on a great battlefield of that war. We have come to dedicate a portion of that field as a final resting place for those who here gave their lives that that nation might live. It is altogether fitting and proper that we should do this. But in a larger sense we cannot dedicate, we cannot hallow this ground. The brave men, living and dead, who struggled here, have consecrated it far above our poor power to add or detract. The world will little note nor long remember what we say here, but it can never forget what they did here. It is for us, the living, rather to be dedicated here to

the unfinished work which they who fought here have thus far so nobly advanced. It is rather for us to be here dedicated to the great task remaining before us, that from these honored dead we take increased devotion to that cause for which they gave the last full measure of devotion; that we here highly resolve that these dead shall not have died in vain, that this nation, under God, shall have a new birth of freedom, and that government of the people, by the people, and for the people, shall not perish from the earth.

This is an introduction to a thought I want to bring to you. I want to call your attention to Daniel's seventy weeks. These weeks are weeks of years, seven years to a week. Daniel's sixty-nine weeks, or 483 days, is dated onward from Daniel and ended with the anointing of Jesus at the River of Jordan. We speak of that anointing as the "Christing of Jesus," when the Holy Ghost from heaven came upon Him. He was then presented to Israel as their Messiah. It required the anointing from heaven to give Him His Messiahship.

Beloved, my soul is dedicated to one purpose, and that is the proclamation of the gospel of the Holy Ghost in our day. If I am left alone in the world as the only voice to declare the full gospel of the Holy Ghost, I will go on declaring it.

Every great movement of God in this world, from the beginning until now, has been an operation of the Holy Ghost. And every fresh introduction of the spirit of man into the life of God has brought a new revelation of Christ and His power to save the world.

Every decline that has followed the history of the Christian church has first had its inception when men began to lie down on the subject of the Holy Ghost. If you want to spell death to an organization that is now alive spiritually, all you have to do is to get them to lie down on the subject of the necessity of the Holy Ghost and the baptism of the Holy Ghost. There will soon be nothing left but a corpse. That is the history of Christianity.

Friends, let us above all else, in the name of Jesus, dedicate ourselves honestly and sincerely to the proclamation of the gospel of the Holy Ghost, of the power of God through the Holy Ghost, to bring into the spirit of man that revelation of Jesus Christ that is essential and final and able to reveal Him as the Son of God.

If that, then, is the one thing to which our souls are dedicated, we will certainly not be slack in our endeavor to seek God for our personal entrance into the life of the Holy Ghost. We will be ready to pray for the baptism of the Holy Ghost. We will be ready to study the Word of God. We will be ready to covet the Holy Ghost and His revelation beyond all else. Out of it come churches. Out of it come preachers. Out of it comes world evangelism. Out of it come high reforms—everything that has its great incentive in the Holy Ghost.

> The greatest thing that Jesus Christ Himself could comprehend as a possibility for mankind was to secure for them the divine right to become the recipients of the Holy Ghost.

The greatest thing that Jesus Christ Himself could comprehend as a possibility for mankind was to secure for them the divine right to become the recipients of the Holy Ghost. And in order to do that, He was compelled to die and shed His blood that their hearts, through its power, should be cleansed from sin and prepared to become the habitation of God through the Spirit.

Lift up your heads, and lift up your hands, and lift up your hearts toward heaven, and declare to the world, the flesh, the devil, and every opposing force in the world that you stand with Jesus Christ for the necessity of the baptism of the Holy Ghost, and that your soul is dedicated to God to carry the precious message wherever you will and, by the grace of God, to minister its eternal power everywhere where God makes it possible! Amen.

16

THE HABITATION OF GOD

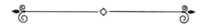

God has been seeking a habitation a long time. God found a habitation in Jesus Christ, and He became the dwelling place of God. Christ's purpose for the world was that men like Himself should become the dwelling place of God. It was not purposed that Jesus Christ was to be a particular or special dwelling place of God. It was rather purposed that mankind should be just as much a holy and desirable dwelling place of God as Jesus Himself was. The purpose of the gospel of God was that through Jesus Christ His Son, many sons should be begotten of God, should be begotten of Christ.

Christ's undertaking was to save mankind from their sins and transform them into sons of God like Himself. That is the purpose and work of our Lord and Savior Jesus Christ.

In the fifteenth chapter of 1 Corinthians, we read of the consummation of His purpose—that is, the finality, the conclusion, of that purpose, when Jesus Himself, having subjected all things unto Himself, is Himself also subjected unto the Father that God may be all in all. There will not be a dissenting voice or a rebellious heart. The will of God has been received, and, as a result of the will of God having been received, there is no longer a necessity for a Savior. Jesus Christ in His capacity of Savior of the world has been completed. His mission is completed.

We are so liable to feel in this great struggle we see about us, and the struggle we recognize in our nature, that there cannot possibly be a time of ultimate and final victory of the Lord Jesus Christ in the souls of men. I want to encourage you, beloved. The Word of God portrays a time and conception of the purpose of Jesus Christ when the world, being redeemed unto Christ, no longer needs the redeeming merit of the Savior. So Jesus, having subjected all things unto Himself, is Himself also subjected unto the Father, that God may be all in all. (See 1 Corinthians 15:28.)

God is not all in all, and He never will be all in all, until the will of God rules in the heart of every man, in the soul of every man—until the redemption of Jesus Christ in its great and ultimate purpose becomes a reality, a finality.

Paul Sees Christ's Purpose

I have always regarded the first and second chapters of Ephesians as two of the most remarkable chapters in the entire Word of God. Perhaps no soul ever envisioned the real purpose of God and portrayed it in words with more clearness than did Paul in these two chapters.

In the first chapter, he begins by showing us that Jesus fulfilled the purpose of the Father. That, as a reward for His consecration to the will of God—His death, resurrection, ascension, and glorification—the power of God ruled in His nature. In truth, He was the Son of God, to whom was committed all power, with principalities and powers being subject unto Him, as Paul said. (See Ephesians 1:21.)

Then, in the second chapter, Paul begins to make this truth applicable to our own heart, and he undertakes to show us that just as Jesus Christ was dead and in the grave, so mankind, possessed and dominated by the powers of sin and selfishness, has become *dead in sin,* that is, senseless to the Spirit of God. (See Ephesians 2:5.) And as Jesus was raised from the dead, so He has purposed to lift the veil or cloud, the obsession or possession of sin, and cleanse the nature of man and unify him with God.

When Paul reaches this climax, he puts it in this terse form: *"For to make in himself of twain one new man, so making peace"* (Ephesians 2:15). He shows that the ultimate and final peace that comes to the soul of man comes as the result of a divine union having taken place between Jesus Christ and the Christian soul, and there is no longer any worry or discussion over commandments or ordinances. The soul has risen above them. It has risen out of the region of commandments and laws into a government of love. The soul joined to Christ in His divine affection, the spirit of man entering into Christ, the Spirit of Christ entering into man, causes such a transformation that the man becomes a new creature. All his impulses have changed, the ruling of his human nature ceases, and finally he is a son of God.

> Jesus purposed to make your heart and mine just as sweet and lovely and pure and holy as His own.

That is the wonder of the cleansing power and the cross of Christ in the nature of man. The wonder is that Jesus purposed to make your heart and mine just as sweet and lovely and pure and holy as His own. That is the reason that He can accept the Christian as His bride. Who could imagine the Christ accepting Christians polluted, defined, of a lower state of purity or holiness than His own?

Interpretation of a Message in Tongues

The Spirit of the Lord says that thus is the wonder of the redemptive power of Jesus Christ revealed to man and in man. Such is the transforming grace that through Him, through His merit, through His love, through His Spirit, the soul of man cleansed, purified, beautified, glorified becomes like the soul of Jesus Himself; and man and Christ meet as equals in purity. Blessed be His name.

If you have felt, dear brother or sister, that you have been a sinner above all that dwelt in Jerusalem, as some did, be assured that the cleansing power of Jesus Christ is equal to your need, and the thoroughness and almightiness of His Spirit's working in you can make you a king and prince, lovely and beautiful, pure of heart and life like unto Himself.

The triumph of the teacher is always in bringing his student to his own understanding and, even more than that, endeavoring to inspire within the student the possibility of going beyond himself in his search of knowledge and truth. Could we expect of Jesus a lesser purpose than that which we recognize in teachers everywhere? If Jesus is a redeemer, unto what is He to redeem us? What is the ideal, what is the standard, to which Christ purposes to bring us? Is the standard less than that which He holds Himself? If so, it would be unworthy of the Son of God. He would not be giving to us the best of His soul.

Truly, the Word of God stands clear in one respect, that *"the blood of Jesus Christ his Son cleanseth us from all sin"* (1 John 1:7). Bless God. We become clean in our nature, thoroughly infilled by His grace, every atom and fiber of the spirit and the soul and the body of man, made sweet and holy, like unto Jesus Himself. Bless God.

The Purpose of Cleansing

Now, this marvelous cleansing by the Spirit and power of Jesus Christ is for a definite purpose; it is a definite preparation. When we make an elaborate preparation of any kind, it is that something may follow. So, this preparation in holiness and righteousness and truth in the nature of man by Jesus Christ, the Word declares, is that there may be a fitting climax; the climax is that man may become the dwelling of God.

God demands a holy temple in which and through which His holiness may be revealed. Consequently, it becomes a matter of necessity to the Lord Jesus Christ that if He is to reveal Himself in a hundredfold measure through the church to the world, He must have the ability to cleanse the church and present her, as the Word portrays, *"not having spot, or wrinkle, or any such thing*" (Ephesians 5:27). Blessed be the Lord. She must be pure as Jesus is pure—beautiful within, beautiful without. The scars and wrinkles must disappear. So Christ will receive the really Christ-cleansed church as His own virgin, the bride. Blessed be the Lord.

The Wonder of His Grace

The wonder of the grace of God is revealed in that, though we have sinned—though we have become polluted, though in our soul-life we have practiced adultery with the spirit of the world until the nature of the world has entered into our nature and soiled it and made it unlike the nature of Jesus Christ—He receives us, cleanses us, purifies us, and saves us. And, being thus redeemed and cleansed by the Spirit of Christ, we stand sweet and lovely and holy in His presence, prepared to be His bride, one in which He can live, with whom He can fellowship, into whose nature He purposes now to come and abide.

The Apostles' Cleansing and Baptism

If you will study with care the life of the apostles, you will observe that there was a process that took place in their lives so thorough and complete that Jesus said unto them, just prior to His departure, "*Now ye are clean through the word which I have spoken unto you*" (John 15:3).

They had arrived in soul cleansing at the place where, by the grace of God, they were prepared for the next experience and higher purpose of Jesus, which was that they might now receive the Holy Ghost. That is, that the Spirit of Jesus Christ might come from heaven to abide in them, and thus in very truth cause them to become the dwelling place of God.

The purpose of Christ was that not only the twelve and the hundred and twenty upon whom the Holy Ghost came at Jerusalem and the church at Samaria and the household of Cornelius should be cleansed and receive the Holy Spirit, but that every son of God should receive a like experience. The church at Samaria was different from the church at

Jerusalem, in that it was composed of the wandering heathen tribes, and it was different from the household of Cornelius, which were intelligent Romans. But they all in common with all the race became the habitation of God through the Spirit.

In common with these, the Ephesian elders in Acts 19 who were advanced in righteousness and holiness and entrusted with the care of others as shepherds of the flock likewise received the Spirit of the Lord.

In all these instances, then, we see that the purpose of God is not only to cleanse a man but, by cleansing him, to empower him, infill him, and indwell him by His own blessed almighty Spirit. The Spirit of Christ present in a holy temple has appeared to reveal Himself through that person, just as He did through the Lord Jesus Christ.

If we study the manner by which the Spirit of God revealed Himself through Jesus, then we will have the pattern or example of how the Spirit of God reveals Himself through all believers all the time.

The Spirit of God spoke through Him the word of love—the word that brought conviction, the word of power. Through His nature there flowed a subtle something that no religionist but Himself and His followers possessed—the living Spirit of the living God, the anointing of the Holy Ghost, bless God, the one characteristic that makes Christianity a distinctive religion forever. It can never be identified with any other. As long as Christianity is dependent on the presence of the Holy Ghost, it will remain distinctively the one religion—that of divine power and saving grace.

Prayer

God, our heavenly Father, our hearts are asking that, since the wondrous provision has been made, we may seek with all the earnestness that should characterize men and women, for this blessed almightiness, that the cleansing grace and power be revealed in our own life. May this not be just a beautiful vision tonight, but, oh Lord, may we receive Thee in this moment into our hearts as our Lord, our Savior, our Redeemer, that the Word of Christ may be accomplished in us and that in very truth we may look into the face of Jesus, knowing that our souls are cleansed. Amen.

When I was a young man, I stood in an aisle of the Methodist church and was introduced to a young lady. As I touched her hand, the marvelous moving of our natures was revealed. Presently, something from her soul, that subtle something that Christians know and recognize as spirit, her spirit, passed to me and went through my person until presently I realized that my soul had rent itself in affection for that woman, and we never had looked into each other's eyes in an intimate way before. From me went that subtle something to her. The result was that we were just as much soul mates and lovers in the next ten minutes as we were in the next seventeen years and had raised a family.

She was a woman of fine sensitive qualities, and she told me later that she had been in the habit of searching a young man's spirit to know if he was pure; but she said, "In your case, the strange thing was that my spirit made no such search. I just knew it." I want to tell you, in that matter she was not wrong, for when I was a boy, though I was surrounded by as vile a set of men as ever lived, I determined in my soul that one day I would look into a woman's soul and tell her that I was pure.

If you held the hand of Jesus tonight, do you suppose your spirit would be capable of searching His soul to know whether He was pure? No, instinctively, something in that purer spirit would cause you to know that it was your Lord.

Then, I want to ask you on the other hand, suppose the Spirit of Jesus searched our own spirit—what would He discern? That is the big question that men are compelled continually to ask of themselves. What would the Spirit of Jesus discern in you? What would the Spirit of Jesus discern in me? Would the Spirit of Jesus be drawn to us, or would we repel Him because of unholiness?

The Word of God lays blessed and splendid emphasis in the fact that we need the cleansing power of Jesus to make our spirit pure and sweet and lovely like His own. Then, having cleansed us and sanctified us to Himself, He Himself, by the Spirit—the Holy Spirit—comes in to dwell in our nature and take up His eternal abiding and residence in us. This we welcome, bless God: the habitation of God through the Spirit.

I sat one day on the platform of a great tabernacle in the presence of ten thousand persons who had collected to hear me preach. I had received a promise from God the night before for that occasion. The Spirit of the Lord had given, in His own words, an outline of the history of man's nature from the creation to the redemption and the empowering by the Spirit of God. But the anointing from heaven that would make possible the presentation of such an ideal and make it acceptable to the hearts of thousands who listened had not yet come.

Presently, from the soul of an old gentleman next to me as I sat praying, I was conscious of the Spirit falling about me until my nature was overcome by it. It was difficult to maintain my seat, waiting for the preliminaries to be finished so that I could get a chance to deliver the message.

That man became the agency of divine transmission of the Spirit of God to me, just the same as Jesus Christ was the agency of divine transmission through which the Spirit of God was imparted to the people of His day.

Such is the marvel of the nature of man united to the Lord Jesus Christ, when all the abundant fullness of His holy nature may come to you and me when our temple has been prepared to receive Him.

Beloved, if you have been getting along with an ounce of healing, bless your soul; if you have been getting along with a limited measure of blessing in your daily life, let me encourage you that the fountain will not be exhausted when your spirit is filled with the overflow.

The Spirit of God is creative, generative, and constructive; the more you give, the more you receive.

The Spirit of God is like the bread that the disciples held in their hands; when it became filled with the Spirit of God, it multiplied in their hands. When they broke off some, there was more remaining than when they began. (See Matthew 14:19–21.) The Spirit of God is creative, generative, and constructive; the more you give, the more you receive. There must be a great opening in the nature of man in order that he may be a large receiver, and the strangeness of it is that it depends upon whether you are large givers. There is nothing like it in the world. It is a violation of every law of man, but it is the common law of the Spirit. Why? Because the Spirit, unlike other things, is creative. It grows, it magnifies in your soul, it multiplies as you distribute it to another.

So Jesus laid down a perpetual law: *"Give, and it shall be given unto you; good measure, pressed down, and shaken together, and running over, shall men give into your bosom"* (Luke 6:38).

In my experience of twenty-five years of healing ministry, I have known very few instances of a person being healed when he approached with such words as these: "If I am healed, I will give the church so much," or "I will make a large donation." You see, the reason is that the Spirit is not received at that place. We are just entering into a knowledge of the law of Jesus Christ: *"Give, and it shall be given unto you."* God tried through the Mosaic law to demonstrate to mankind that the way of blessing was the way of giving. See old Isaac when he approached God, coming with his lamb or dove in his hand, or whatever the sacrifice was that he was about to offer on his behalf.

The Christian's Offering

But, beloved, Christianity has a deeper revelation of the same truth. We come, not with a dove or a lamb or a he-goat or a heifer. No, we come with our life, we come with our nature, we come with our all, offering it to the Lord—not bargaining with Him; not endeavoring by a shrewd bargain to obtain the blessing. That is the reason many a soul loses its blessing. Quit it.

Very rarely have I known people to miss the blessing of God when they came openly, saying, "I desire to receive; I want to give." Their spirit, their nature, has come into harmony with God's law that says, *"Give, and it shall be given unto you."* Don't you know, that is the secret of all affection between man and man, between the sexes? Men are not always seeking for someone to love them; they are seeking for someone they can love. When two souls are seeking for the one they can love, there is a union, and the world very gradually is learning that there are real marriages. There is a union of spirit so indissoluble that nothing on earth or in heaven will ever sunder it.

Christ is seeking for the soul that will receive His love, and the Christian, the real one, is seeking for the Christ who will receive his love. Bless God. Both are practicing this unalterable law of God: *"Give, and it shall be given unto you."*

Frequently, we observe that sympathy becomes the door through which affection enters lives. I once talked with a nurse, and I asked her what the hardest thing in a nurse's life was. She said, "If you remain a woman and do not become steeled in your nature and hardened in your affections, you will find it most difficult to keep from permitting your affections to follow your sympathy." Over and over, as a law of life, a woman will nurse a man, and before she is through, she will love him. Why? Because sympathy for him has opened the door of her nature and unconsciously has flowed out in affection to him.

There is one thing that is dearer to God than anything else, and the only thing that is worthwhile. It is the same thing that is dearer to every man. That thing is the affection of your heart. You can see your son rise to a place of eminence and respect in the world, and yet he will disappoint your soul. Why? Because the soul of the real father is seeking something besides that. He is seeking the affection of the son, and if he fails to receive it, all the rest is barren.

Christ is seeking the affection of mankind, the union of their spirit with His, for without their affection there can never be that deep union of the spirit between God and man that makes possible a richness of life made glorious by His indwelling. That is why the love of God is held forth in the Word as the one supreme attraction to draw the soul of man in returned affection.

And you can give to your Lord your money and your property and your brain and all the other things that are usually considered to be very excellent, but if you withhold your affections from Him and give them to another, the Word says you are an adulterer.

Prayer

Our Father, teach us to love Thee; teach us, dear Lord, its value; teach us its power; teach us our spirit's need. My God, in the richness of Thy beautiful Spirit, all the impoverished nature's need is supplied. In turn, if we can add to Thy joy by giving to Thee the affection of our heart, great God, who could withhold? Amen.

As long as religion exists, you will never be able to separate real religion from the emotions of the soul. The emotions will be an open door which the Spirit uses to gain access to your life. When you reduce religious life to a science and take from it the warmth of Christ's affection, you have robbed of its charm and its almighty power.

God in Man's Mind

When we become the habitation of God—when God lives in the mind and in the brain—what will be the result? What will we do, and what will we say or think? What will be the tenderness of our emotions, of our soul, and what will be the depth of our feeling? What will be the growth of our capacity to love?

God in Man's Spirit

When God lives in a man's spirit, the spirit of man reaches out into the boundless, touching the almightiness of God, discerning His nature, appropriating His power, and securing His almightiness.

God in a Man's Body

God living in a man's flesh, giving off a vibration of God-life, God-power—God indwelling his blood, God indwelling his hands, God indwelling his bones and marrow—makes him a habitation of God.

A real Christian woman will keep her heart clean and calm; a real Christian man will take a bath as often as he needs it and a lot of other things. Otherwise, he has a poor conception of the Son of God, who inhabits man. He will be beautiful within, beautiful without. You cannot retain the dirt and filth and rottenness and Jesus Christ at the same time. But if there begins a mighty war in your nature, the Spirit of God striving with devils, and God overcomes, then you will understand the power and redemption of Christ.

I was present in a meeting in Los Angeles one time when the Spirit fell on a man, he fell prostrate on the floor, and a group of friends gathered around. He would fight like a mad dog until he would actually swear. In the next two or three minutes, that spirit would be overpowered by the Spirit of God, and he would be a saint and cry for help. Again that evil spirit would come into evidence.

The brethren said, "Mr. Lake, why don't you cast the devil out?" I replied, "God wants someone else at that job." So we sat until four in the morning. At two minutes till four, the evil spirit departed, and the glory of God broke forth, and the worship of the man, when he recognized his Lord, was wonderfully sacred. The man arose, transformed by the indwelling of the living God.

Beloved, I want to say that if any unholiness exists in the nature, it is not by the consent of the Spirit of God. If unholiness exists in your life, it is because your soul is giving consent to it, and you are retaining it. Let it go. Get it out and let God have His way in your life.

Prayer

> God my Father, as we kneel tonight, some may feel and do feel the Spirit of God upon them to overpower and cast out every unholy thing. Lord God, we are glad that Christ made this divine provision for our deliverance. We would be Thine. We would be Thine alone. We would be Thine forever and forever. It is not that we may come to heaven when we die. We put away that littleness and that selfishness from our minds; and it is not, Lord God, that we may escape from punishment, for, God, we put away that devilish littleness. We would be Thine because it is worthy of a son of God to be like his Lord. We would be Thine because we have desired to join our hands and hearts in the biggest miracle the world ever knew—the redemption of the race to God forever. Father God, with such a vision we look to Thee, asking that by Thy grace Thee cleanse our hearts and make us indeed the dwelling place of God. Amen.

The triumph of the gospel is enough to make any man the wildest kind of an enthusiastic optimist.

Man in God and God in man—one mind, one purpose, one power, one glory. The unifying of the nature of man and God is the crowning achievement of Jesus.

PART V

SANCTIFICATION AND
CONSECRATION

17

A TRUMPET CALL

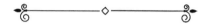

1908
Johannesburg, South Africa

The thirteenth chapter of Acts tells us the story of the ordination and sending forth of the apostle Paul—his ordination to the apostleship. Paul never identified himself as an apostle until after the thirteenth chapter of Acts. He had been an evangelist and a teacher for thirteen years when Acts chapter 13 was written and when the ordination that is recorded there took place. Men who have a real call are not afraid of apprenticeships.

There is a growing up in experience in the ministry. When Paul started out in the ministry, he was definitely called of God and was assured of God through Ananias that it would not be an easy service but a terrific one. God said to Ananias:

Arise, and go into the street which is called Straight, and inquire in the house of Judas for one called Saul, of Tarsus: for, behold, he prayeth. …He is a chosen vessel unto me, to bear my name before the

Gentiles, and kings, and the children of Israel: for I will show him
how great things he must suffer for my name's sake.

(Acts 9:11, 15–16)

That is what Jesus Christ, the crucified and glorified Son of God,
told Ananias to say to the apostle Paul. He was not going to live in a holy
ecstasy and wear a beautiful halo and have a heavenly time and ride in a
limousine. He was going to have a drastic time, a desperate struggle, a
terrific experience. And no man in biblical history ever had more dread-
ful things to endure than the apostle Paul. He gave a list in his letter to
the Corinthians of the things he had endured.

Of the Jews five times received I forty stripes save one. Thrice was
I beaten with rods, once was I stoned, thrice I suffered shipwreck,
a night and a day I have been in the deep; in journeyings often, in
perils of waters, in perils of robbers, in perils by mine own country-
men, in perils by the heathen, in perils in the city, in perils in the
wilderness, in perils in the sea, in perils among false brethren; in
weariness and painfulness, in watchings often, in hunger and thirst,
in fastings often, in cold and nakedness.

(2 Corinthians 11:24–27)

They stripped him of his clothing, and the executioner lashed him
with an awful scourge, until, bleeding and lacerated and broken, he fell
helpless and unconscious and insensible. Then, they doused him with a
bucket of salt water to keep the maggots off and threw him into a cell to
recover. That was the price of apostleship. That was the price of the call
of God and His service. But God said that Paul would *"bear my name*
before the Gentiles, and kings, and the children of Israel" (Acts 9:15). Paul
qualified as God's messenger.

Beloved, we have lost the character of consecration here manifested.
God is trying to restore it in our day. He has not been able to make
much progress with the average preacher on that line. "Mrs. So-and-so
said thus and such, and I am just not going to take it." That is the kind of
preacher with another kind of call, not the heaven call, not the God call,

not the death call if necessary. That is not the kind of call the apostle Paul had.

Do you want to know why God poured out His Spirit in South Africa like He did nowhere else in the world? There was a reason. This example will illustrate. We had one hundred twenty-five men out on the field at one time. We were a very young institution; were not known in the world. South Africa is seven thousand miles from any European country. It is ten thousand miles by way of England to the United States. Our finances got so low under the awful assault we were compelled to endure that there came a time I could not even mail to these workers at the end of the month a ten-dollar bill. It got so that I could not send them two dollars. The situation was desperate. What was I to do? Under these circumstances, I did not want to take the responsibility of leaving men and their families on the frontier without real knowledge of what the conditions were.

Some of us at headquarters sold our clothes in some cases, sold certain pieces of furniture out of the house, sold anything we could sell, to bring those hundred twenty-five workers off the field for a conference.

One night in the progress of the conference, I was invited by a committee to leave the room for a minute or two. The conference attendees wanted to have a word by themselves. So, I stepped out to a restaurant for a cup of coffee and came back. When I came in, I found they had rearranged the chairs in an oval, with a little table at one end, and on the table were the bread and the wine. Old Father Van der Wall, speaking for the company, said, "Brother Lake, during your absence, we have come to a conclusion. We have made our decision. We want you to serve the Lord's Supper. We are going back to our fields. We are going back if we have to walk back. We are going back if we have to starve. We are going back if our wives die. We are going back if our children die. We are going back if we die ourselves. We have but one request: If we die, we want you to come and bury us."

The next year, I buried twelve men and sixteen wives and children. In my judgment, not one of the twelve, if they had had a few things that a man needs to eat, might not have died. Friends, when you want to find out why the power of God came down from heaven in South Africa like it never came down before since the times of the apostles, there is your answer.

Jesus Christ put the spirit of martyrdom in the ministry. Jesus instituted His ministry with a pledge unto death. When He was with the disciples on the last night, He took the cup and gave it to them, after He drank, "*saying….*" Beloved, the saying was the significant thing. It was Jesus Christ's pledge to the twelve who stood with Him, "This cup is the New Testament in My blood; '*drink ye all of it*'" (Matthew 26:27).

Friends, those who were there and drank to that pledge of Jesus Christ entered into the same covenant and purpose that He did. That is what all pledges mean. Men have pledged themselves in the wine cup from time immemorial. Generals have pledged their armies unto death. It has been a custom in the race. Jesus Christ sanctified it to the church forever. Bless God.

"'*Drink ye all of it; for this is my blood of the new testament*' (Matthew 26:27). Let us become one. Let us become one in our purpose to die for the world. Your blood and Mine together. '*My blood of the new testament.*' It is My demand from you. It is your high privilege."

Dear friends, there is not an authentic history that can tell us whether any one of them died a natural death. We know that at least nine of them were martyrs, possibly all. Peter died on a cross; James was beheaded; for Thomas they did not even wait to make a cross—they nailed him to an olive tree. John was sentenced to be executed at Ephesus by being placed in a cauldron of boiling oil. God delivered him, and his executioners refused to repeat the operation, so he was banished to the Isle of Patmos. John thought so little about it that he never even told of the incident. He said, "I…*was in the isle that is called Patmos, for the word of God, and for the testimony of Jesus Christ*" (Revelation 1:9). That was explanation enough. He had committed himself to Jesus Christ for life or death.

Friends, the group of missionaries who followed me went without food and went without clothes; and, once, when one of my preachers was suffering from sunstroke and had wandered away, I tracked him by the bloody marks of his footprints. Another time I was hunting for one of my missionaries, a young Englishman, twenty-two years of age. He had come from a lineage of Church of England preachers for five hundred years. When I arrived at the native village, the old native chief said, "He is not here. He went over the mountains; but you know, mister, he is a white man and has not learned to walk barefooted."

> "He is not here. He went over the mountains; but you know, mister, he is a white man and has not learned to walk barefooted."

That is the kind of consecration that established Pentecost in South Africa. That is the reason we have a hundred thousand native Christians in South Africa. That is the reason we have 1,250 native preachers. That is the reason we have 350 white churches in South Africa. That is the reason that today we are the most rapidly growing church in South Africa.

I am not persuading you, dear friends, by holding out a hope that the way is going to be easy. I am calling you in the name of Jesus Christ, you dear ones who expect to be ordained to the gospel of Jesus Christ tonight, to take the route that Jesus took, the route that the apostles took, the route that the early church took—the victory route, whether by life or death. Historians declare, "The blood of the martyrs was the seed of the church." Beloved, that is what the difficulty is in our day— we have so little seed. The church needs more martyr blood.

If I were pledging men and women to the gospel of the Son of God, as I am endeavoring to do tonight, it would not be to have a nice church and harmonious surroundings and a sweet, do-nothing time. I would invite them to be ready to die. That was the spirit of early Methodism. John Wesley established a heroic call. He demanded every preacher to be "ready to pray, ready to preach, ready to die." That is always the spirit of Christianity. When any other spirit comes into the church, it is not the spirit of Christianity. It is a foreign spirit. It is a sissified substitute.

I lived on cornmeal mush many a time with my family, and we did not grumble, and I preached to thousands of people, not poor colored people, but well-off white people. When my missionaries were on the field existing on cornmeal mush, I could not eat pie. My heart was joined to them. That is the reason we never had splits in our work in South Africa, the one country where Pentecost never split. The split business began to develop years afterward, when pumpkin-pie-eating Pentecostal missionaries began infesting the country. Men who are ready to die for the Son of God do not split. They do not holler the first time they get a stomachache.

Bud Robinson tells a story of himself. He went to preach in the southern mountains. It was the first time in his life that no one invited him to go home and eat with him. So, he slept on the floor that night— and the next night and the next night. After five days and five nights had passed, and his stomach began to growl for food terribly, every once in a while he would stop and say, "Lay down, you brute!" and go on with his sermon. That is what won. That is what will win every time. That is what we need today. We need men who are willing to get off the highway. When I started to preach the gospel, I walked twenty miles on Sunday morning to my service and walked home twenty miles in the night when I got through. I did it for years for Jesus and souls.

In early Methodism, an old local preacher would start out on Saturday and walk all night and then walk all Sunday night to get back to his work. It was the common custom. Peter Cartwright preached for sixty dollars per year and baptized ten thousand converts.

Friends, we talk about consecration, and we preach about consecration, but that is the kind of consecration that my heart is asking for tonight. That is the kind of consecration that will get answers from heaven. That is the kind God will honor. That is the consecration to which I would pledge Pentecost. I would strip Pentecost of its frills and folderol. Jesus Christ, through the Holy Ghost, calls us tonight not to an earthly mansion and a ten-thousand-dollar motorcar, but to put our lives—body and soul and spirit—on the altar of service. All hail, you who are ready to die for Christ and this glorious Pentecostal gospel! We salute you. You are brothers with us and with your Lord.

18

HOLINESS UNTO THE LORD

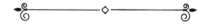

March 6, 1916
Spokane, Washington

Holiness is the character of God. The very substance of His being and essence of His nature is purity. The purpose of God in the salvation of mankind is to produce in man a kindred holiness, a radiant purity, like unto that of God Himself. If God were unable to produce in him such a purity, then His purpose in man would be a failure, and the object of the sacrifice of Jesus Christ would be a miscarriage instead of a triumph.

The triumph of Jesus Christ was attained through His willingness to be led by the Spirit of God. The triumph of the Christian can be attained only in a similar manner. Even though God has baptized a soul with the Holy Spirit, there yet remains, as with Jesus, the present necessity of walking in humility and permitting the Spirit of God to be his absolute guide.

The unveiling of consciousness, of the desire of the flesh, of the sensuality of the nature and the thought of man, the revelation of adverse tendencies, is part of God's purpose and necessary for growth in God.

How can the nature of man be changed except that nature is first revealed? So there arises in the heart the desire and prayer for the Spirit of God to eject, crucify, and destroy every tendency of opposition to the Holy Spirit. Think not that thou shalt attain the highest in God until within thine own soul a heavenly longing to be like Him who gave His life for us possesses thine heart.

Think not to come within the court of God with stain upon your garments. Think not that heaven can smile upon a nature fouled through evil contact. Think not that Christ can dwell in temples seared by flames of hate. No! The heart of man must first be purged by holy fire and washed from every stain by cleansing blood. Don't you know that he whose nature is akin to God's must ever feel the purging power of Christ within?

He who would understand the ways of God must trust the Spirit's power to guide and keep. He who would tread the paths where angels tread himself must realize seraphic purity. Such is the nature of God, such the working of the Spirit's power, such the attainment of him who overcomes. In him the joy and power of God shall be. Through him the healing streams of life shall flow. To him heaven's gates are opened wide. In him the kingdom is revealed.

Interpretation of a Message in Tongues

Fear not to place thy hand within the nail-pierced palm. Fear not to trust His guidance. The way He trod is marked by bleeding feet and wet with many tears. He leadeth thee aright, and heaven's splendor soon shall open to thy spirit, and thou shalt know that all triumphant souls—those who have overcome indeed—have found their entrance by this path into the realms of light.

19

SANCTIFICATION

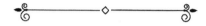

Scripture Reading: 1 Thessalonians 5

But of the times and the seasons, brethren, ye have no need that I write unto you. For yourselves know perfectly that the day of the Lord so cometh as a thief in the night. For when they shall say, Peace and safety; then sudden destruction cometh upon them, as travail upon a woman with child; and they shall not escape. But ye, brethren, are not in darkness, that that day should overtake you as a thief. Ye are all the children of light, and the children of the day: we are not of the night, nor of darkness. Therefore let us not sleep, as do others; but let us watch and be sober. For they that sleep sleep in the night; and they that be drunken are drunken in the night. But let us, who are of the day, be sober, putting on the breastplate of faith and love; and for an helmet, the hope of salvation. For God hath not appointed us to wrath, but to obtain salvation by our Lord Jesus Christ, Who died for us, that, whether we wake or sleep, we should live together with him. Wherefore comfort yourselves together, and edify one another, even as also ye do. And we beseech you, brethren, to know them which labour among you, and are over you in the Lord, and admonish you; And to esteem them very highly in love for their work's sake. And be at peace among yourselves. Now we exhort you, brethren, warn them that are unruly, comfort the feebleminded, support the weak, be patient toward all men. See that none render evil for evil unto any man; but ever follow that which is good, both among yourselves, and to all men. Rejoice evermore. Pray without ceasing. In every thing give thanks: for this is the will of God in Christ Jesus concerning you. Quench not the Spirit. Despise not prophesyings. Prove all things; hold fast that which is good. Abstain from all appearance of evil. And the very God of peace sanctify you wholly; and I pray God your whole spirit and soul and body be preserved blameless unto the coming of our Lord Jesus Christ. Faithful is he that calleth you, who also will do it. Brethren, pray for us. Greet all the brethren with an holy kiss. I charge you by the Lord that this epistle be read unto all the holy brethren. The grace of our Lord Jesus Christ be with you. Amen.   (1 Thessalonians 5:1–28)

Beloved, the thought that is in my spirit tonight is the truth from the words we have just read, the sanctification of spirit and soul and body. Paul said,

> *I pray God your whole spirit and soul and body be preserved blameless unto the coming of our Lord Jesus Christ. Faithful is he that calleth you, who also will do it.*   (Hebrews 4:12)

Most of us in our reading of the Scriptures have this difficulty, and it is a perfectly natural one, of recognizing body and soul only. And man is generally spoken of as a duality of body and soul. However, the Scriptures do not recognize man as a dual being, but a triune being like Himself.

Therefore, the apostle said, "*I pray God your whole spirit and soul and body be preserved blameless unto the coining of our Lord Jesus Christ.*"

One difficulty we have in the study of this subject is that in the common translation of our English Bible there is very little distinction made between soul and spirit. It is one of the most difficult things in the world to express the common truths we teach in another language. Paul coined seventeen distinct words in his letter to the Ephesians to express the fine distinctions of soul and spirit.

Paul declared in the book of Hebrews the possibility of divisibility of soul and spirit. He says:

For the word of God is quick, and powerful, and sharper than any two-edged sword, piercing even to the dividing asunder of soul and spirit, and of the joints and marrow, and is a discerner of the thoughts and intents of the heart. (1 Thessalonians 5:23–24)

Beloved, the spirit of man is a great unknown realm in the lives of most men. My judgment is that the spirit lies dormant in most men until quickened by the living Spirit of God and until fertilized by the real Spirit of Jesus Christ. But when touched by the Spirit of God, a quickening takes place. The spirit of man comes into activity and begins to operate within him. It not only discerns things in this life, like the spirit of another, or in another, but it reaches way beyond this present life and becomes that medium by which we touch God Himself and by which we know and comprehend heavenly things.

In my judgment, the spirit of man is the most amazing instrument of God that there is in all the world. We have this declaration in the book of Job concerning man's spirit:

There is a spirit in man: and the inspiration of the Almighty giveth them understanding. (Job 32:8)

When a soul comes to God and surrenders his life to Him we say he is converted, and by that we mean changed, born again of God so that the common things which were evident in his life as a fleshly being fell away and were gone, and the spiritual life appeared in him, and in the truest sense he began his walk as a child of God.

I believe a real conversion is the awakening of the spirit of man to the consciousness of the Fatherhood of God through Jesus Christ. In order to be aware of that consciousness of union with God, it is necessary that everything be removed that hides that consciousness and dims the knowledge of God.

Sin is that peculiar thing in the life of man which dims the consciousness of man so he cannot comprehend God. When sin is removed, the veil over the soul of man is gone and the spirit of man looks into the face of God and recognizes that God is his Father through the Lord Jesus Christ. Bless God, the spirit of man ascending into union with God brings into our soul the consciousness that God is our all and in all.

The soul of man is that intermediate quality between body and spirit. The soul, in other words, comprehends all the action of our mental powers—the natural mind. The soul of man is that which reaches out and takes possession of the knowledge that the spirit has attained and expresses that knowledge through the outer man. The soul of man is the governing power in the constitution of man.

I feel in my heart that one of the things we need to learn very much is this; that the soul of man, not the spirit, has a marvelous power.

If I were to endeavor to define in terms I feel the people would understand, I would speak of the action of the soul of man as that which is commonly spoken of by students as the subconscious. As you read the writings of psychic authors, you will observe the actions and powers they define are not the powers of the spirit in union with God but the action of the soul of man. The soul of man is the real ego. When the Word of God speaks of the salvation of the soul it speaks in truly scientific language. For unless the soul, the mind of man, is redeemed from his own self into the Spirit of God that man is, in my judgment, still an unredeemed man.

Sanctification is calculated to apply to the needs of all our nature, first of the spirit, second of the soul, third of the body. Over and over again I have repeated those blessed words of John Wesley in his definition of sanctification. He said: "Sanctification is possessing the mind of Christ, and all the mind of Christ."

> "Sanctification is possessing the mind of Christ, and all the mind of Christ."

The ultimate of entire sanctification would comprehend all the mind of Christ. Christians are usually very weak in this department of their nature. Perhaps less pains have been taken by Christians to develop their mind in God than almost anything else.

We pay attention particularly to one thing only—the spirit—and we do not comprehend the fact that God purposed that the things God's Spirit brings to us shall be applied in a practical manner to the needs of our present life.

I was absolutely shocked the other day beyond anything I think my spirit ever received. A dear lady who professes not only to live a holy life but to possess the real baptism of the Holy Ghost and who discusses the subject a great deal, was guilty of saying one of the vilest things I ever heard concerning another. I said in my own soul that individual has not even discerned the outer fringes of what sanctification by the Spirit of God means. I do not believe there is even an evidence of sanctification in that life. Certainly a mind that could repeat such a damning thing gives no evidence whatever but of a very superficial knowledge of God, very superficial indeed.

It shows us this thing: that people are placing their dependence in the fact that in their spirit they know God, that they have been saved from sin, and are going to heaven when they die; but they are living like the devil in this present life, talking like the devil. It is an abomination. It spells a tremendous degree of ignorance. It shows that that individual does not comprehend the first principles of the breadth of salvation as Jesus taught it to the world—a holy mind, a sanctified spirit.

Beloved, I tell you with all candor, a holy mind cannot repeat a vile thing let alone be the creator of the vile suggestion. It is an unholy mind that is capable of such an act. And I say with Paul, mark such a person. Put your finger on him. Just note it. He can talk, but he does not know God. He does not comprehend the power of His salvation.

But bless God, here is the hope, here is the strength, here is the power of the gospel of Jesus Christ—that the power of God unto salvation applied to the mind of man sanctifies the soul of man and makes the mind of man like the mind of Christ.

Who could imagine from the lips of Jesus an unholy suggestion that would jar the spirit of another? The mind could not conceive of such a thing. Never could the mind conceive ought from God but the outflow of a holy life, quickening his mind, infilling it with love and purity and peace and power.

Beloved, in our home, in our life, in our office, wherever we are, we leave the impression of our thoughts there. If our thoughts are pure and holy like Christ, people will walk into the atmosphere and instantly discover it.

Prayer

> God, I pray that the power of God will come upon the Christian people, that they may feel, O God, the necessity of submitting the wicked, accursed, vile mind of man to the living God to be purged and cleansed and remolded, that it may become in deed and in truth the mind of Christ.

If there is any particular place in our lives where as a rule Christians are weak, it is in the consecration of their minds. Christians seem to feel as if they were not to exercise any control over the mind and so it seems to run at random, just like the mind of the world.

Real Christianity is marked by the pureness, by the holiness of the thoughts of man, and if Christianity—the kind you have—does not produce in your mind real holiness, real purity, real sweetness, real truth, then it is a poor brand. Change it right away.

> Real Christianity is marked by the pureness,
> by the holiness of the thoughts of man.

Beloved, there is relief for such; there is a way of salvation. It is in the submission of that mind to the Lord Jesus to be remolded by the Holy Spirit so that that mind becomes the pure channel of a holy nature.

Beloved, surely we who profess to know the living God, who profess to live in union with Him, ought to present to the world that attitude of mind, that pureness of mind, that holiness of mind which needs no recommendation. The people know it, they feel it, they smell it. They know it is the mind of Christ. I love that definition of John Wesley's which says, "Possessing the mind of Christ and all the mind of Christ."

Prayer

O God, I ask Thee that Thou wilt help me and the soul of this people to submit our minds to God so that they may be remolded in love and sweetness and purity and holiness, so that in the name of Jesus they are the minds of Christ.

Beloved, we are going a step further—the effect of a pure mind on the body of man and in the flesh of man. Do you know that the sins of vileness in men's lives originate in the mind? A man's life will be of the character of his thought. If he thinks evil he will be evil. If he thinks holy he will be holy. His outward life will be as the inner impulse is. Jesus said,

From within, out of the heart of men, proceed evil thoughts, adul-
teries, fornications, murders, thefts, covetousness, wickedness, deceit,
lasciviousness, an evil eye, blasphemy, pride, foolishness: all these evil
things come from within, and defile the man. (Mark 7:21–23)

They were troubled because Jesus and the disciples were eating and drinking from dishes which were not ceremonially cleansed. Jesus was trying to teach the great lesson of the deep and inner life. He said, "Out of the heart come evil things."

"That which goes into the mouth cannot defile a man." (See Mark 7:18.)

Beloved, our minds need to be stayed in Christ, kept by the power of God, infilled with the Holy Spirit of Christ so that we reflect His beauty, we show forth His love, we manifest His sweetness, and we evidence His power.

Long ago I learned this splendid lesson. One night I was in a strange city and was sick. I wanted somebody to pray for me. A person was present, and he suggested that he would pray. I knelt by a chair on the floor, and he put his hands on me, and I arose from that chair with one of the most tremendous passions in my nature, one of the most terrible conditions of sensuousness in me. It was days before I felt that I got back again where I was pure and holy in the sight of God. I did not understand it at the time, but afterward that individual came to me with the confession of the character of his life, and I understood then. I received the condition of that nature, and in my receptive attitude I received of the vileness of that person in my nature. It seemed my soul was soiled for days in consequence.

That taught me, beloved, to be careful who laid their hands on me. After that, I waited until the Spirit of the living God indicated in my soul that the person who offered to perform such a ministry was pure.

Isn't it marvelous, beautiful, wonderful to realize that mankind can receive into their nature and being the power and spirit of the living Christ, which contains the purging power to drive forth from the being every particle of evil, every sensuous thing in the thought and nature so that the man becomes what Jesus was. That is what the blood of Jesus Christ is calculated to do. That is what the spirit of Christ is purposed to do in the soul of a man—the cleansing of a nature from the power and dominion of sin.

Beloved, the inflow of holy life into our body must produce holiness in the body, just as it does in the soul. We cannot even think beautiful thoughts, we cannot think holy thoughts, without them leaving their impression in our nature, in our very flesh.

That same divine power in us dissolves disease, restores diseased tissues. Our flesh is purged by the divine power being transmitted from our spirit, through our soul, into our body.

I have always loved to think of the holy flesh of Jesus, not just His beautiful mind, not just the pure Spirit; but is it not blessed and sweet to contemplate the flesh cleansed and purified until His very body—His hands, His feet, His person—were just as pure by the Spirit of God as His pure soul and His pure Spirit were.

That is why Jesus was the wonderful channel He was. The Spirit of God would flow through Him just as freely, just as fully, just as powerfully as it was possible for it to flow through a holy, purified personality.

I like to contemplate the Lord Jesus on the Mount of Transfiguration and think of the radiant glory that came through His flesh, not just the illumination of His spirit, but the holy glory emanating through His flesh until He became white and glistening, until His clothes were white and His face shown as the light. It is that radiant purity of God that my soul covets. It is that radiant power, evidenced in the pureness of my spirit, my mind, my very flesh that I long for.

So beloved, we see that when something impure, of the character of disease, appears on your flesh and mine and we feel we are being soiled by an unholy touch, in the name of Jesus our spirit reaches up and rebukes that devilish condition, and by the Spirit of the living God we stand, believing that the Holy Spirit of God will flow through the spirit, flow through the soul, through the flesh, and remedy and heal that difficulty that is in the person.

An old Baptist brother was in to see me about his wife. As I sat reasoning with him, I said, "Brother, I would just as soon have my brother commit a sin as to have sickness in his person. One is the evidence of an impure mind, the other is the evidence of an impure body. And the salvation of Jesus was intended to make him pure in spirit, in soul, and in body."

> *I pray God your whole spirit and soul and body be preserved blameless unto the coming of our Lord Jesus Christ. Faithful is he that calleth you who also will do it.*   (1 Thessalonians 5:23–24)

There is a stream of life that God permits to flow from your nature and mine to all men everywhere. That blessed stream will be either sweet and pure as the stream that flows from the throne of God, or it will be soiled and foul according to the condition of our nature. The value of the precious blood of Jesus Christ to you and me is that through it that life stream that flows from us may be made holy—that same holy living life-stream that causes the Tree of Life to bloom.

Of all the pictures that the Word of God contains, the one described in Revelation 22 is the most beautiful:

> *He shewed me a pure river of water of life, clear as crystal, proceeding out of the throne of God and of the Lamb. In the midst of the street of it, and on either side of the river, was there the tree of life, which bare twelve manner of fruits, and yielded her fruit every month: and the leaves of the tree were for the healing of the nations. And there shall be no more curse: but the throne of God and of the Lamb shall be in it; and his servants shall serve him: And they shall see his face; and his name shall be in their foreheads. And there shall be no night there; and they need no candle, neither light of the sun; for the Lord God giveth them light: and they shall reign for ever and ever. And he said unto me, These sayings are faithful and true: and the Lord*

God of the holy prophets sent his angel to shew unto his servants the things which must shortly be done. Behold, I come quickly: blessed is he that keepeth the sayings of the prophecy of this book. And I John saw these things, and heard them. And when I had heard and seen, I fell down to worship before the feet of the angel which shewed me these things. Then saith he unto me, See thou do it not: for I am thy fellowservant, and of thy brethren the prophets, and of them which keep the sayings of this book: worship God. And he saith unto me, Seal not the sayings of the prophecy of this book: for the time is at hand. He that is unjust, let him be unjust still: and he which is filthy, let him be filthy still: and he that is righteous, let him be righteous still: and he that is holy, let him be holy still. And, behold, I come quickly; and my reward is with me, to give every man according as his work shall be. I am Alpha and Omega, the beginning and the end, the first and the last. Blessed are they that do his command-ments, that they may have right to the tree of life, and may enter in through the gates into the city. For without are dogs, and sorcerers, and whoremongers, and murderers, and idolaters, and whosoever loveth and maketh a lie. I Jesus have sent mine angel to testify unto you these things in the churches. I am the root and the offspring of David, and the bright and morning star. And the Spirit and the bride say, Come. And let him that heareth say, Come. And let him that is athirst come. And whosoever will, let him take the water of life freely. For I testify unto every man that heareth the words of the prophecy of this book, If any man shall add unto these things, God shall add unto him the plagues that are written in this book: And if any man shall take away from the words of the book of this proph-ecy, God shall take away his part out of the book of life, and out of the holy city, and from the things which are written in this book. He which testifieth these things saith, Surely I come quickly. Amen. Even so, come, Lord Jesus. The grace of our Lord Jesus Christ be with you all. Amen. (Revelation 22:1–21)

Beloved, if your life has not been satisfactory, if you have not recog-nized the holy character that Christ expects from a real Christian, then this call of the Spirit comes to your soul. *"The Spirit and the bride say come."* Come up, come into the real life, the high life, the life hid with Christ in God.

Jesus has promised us, "I will be within thee a well of water, springing up into everlasting life." (See John 4:14.)

20

THE HIGHWAY OF HOLINESS

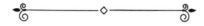

January 10, 1922
Hillside, Oregon

Say to them that are of a fearful heart, Be strong, fear not: behold, your God will come with vengeance, even God with a recompense; he will come and save you. Then the eyes of the blind shall be opened, and the ears of the deaf shall be unstopped. Then shall the lame man leap as an hart, and the tongue of the dumb sing: for in the wilderness shall waters break out, and streams in the desert. And the parched ground shall become a pool, and the thirsty land springs of water: in the habitation of dragons, where each lay, shall be grass with reeds and rushes. And an highway shall be there, and a way, and it shall be called the way of holiness; the unclean shall not pass over it; but it shall be for those: the wayfaring men, though fools, shall not err therein. No lion shall be there, nor any ravenous beast shall go up thereon, it shall not be found there; but the redeemed shall walk there: and the ransomed of the LORD shall return, and come to Zion with songs and everlasting joy upon their heads: they shall

234 *The Flow of the Spirit*

obtain joy and gladness, and sorrow and sighing shall flee away.
(Isaiah 35:4–10)

T he eyes of the blind shall be opened" (Isaiah 35:5). Once, I was acquainted with a cartoonist who illustrated this very clearly. He pictured three scenes representing the three themes of that chapter. The three themes are:

+ Salvation

+ Healing

+ Holiness

Representing the first theme, a man is kneeling, and all around him are the scenes of his life, represented by different animals. The man is kneeling, bowed in prayer for salvation, and presently the great hand of God is just extended down to pick him up and is in the act of lifting him up. That is *salvation.*

The second theme, healing, is represented by a man standing on crutches. Just above his head was the hand of God. He was reaching to get hold of that hand, and in his effort to do so he forgot his crutches, and they fell this way and that way, and presently the man was walking after the hand. That is faith. That is *healing.*

The third theme is represented by the same individual walking along a highway on which the flowers were blooming and the pleasant waters flowing and down in the distance was the light of eternal glory. And as he went he sang. That is the highway of *holiness.*

No lion shall be there, nor any ravenous beast shall go up thereon, it shall not be found there; but the redeemed shall walk there.
(Isaiah 35:9)

That is the Christian's state. That is the normal soul state. Christians as a rule are covered with shadows, with fears, and doubts. That is not the realm of God at all. That is the realm of darkness.

Christianity lives in the light. Christianity lives in the glory. Christianity lives in the power of God, in the eternal presence of God. And it is that consciousness of God and union with Him that gives to the soul strength and assurance and confidence and helps the soul to go on its way, regardless of conditions and circumstances, so that he is not being governed by this thing or that, but by the faith of God. Instead of conditions controlling him, he is controlling conditions. That is the power of God.

A dwarf never needs to be measured for his clothes, but a growing boy outgrows his clothes.   —*Kernahan*

21

THE POWER OF CONSECRATION TO PRINCIPLE

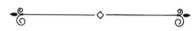

The successful Christian life rests on three essentials:

+ First: A knowledge of the teaching of the Lord and Savior Jesus Christ, whose words are the final authority, the bar where every question must be brought for final decision. The words of every other must be measured, and their value determined, by the statements of Jesus Christ. *"In him dwelleth all the fulness of the Godhead bodily"* (Colossians 2:9).

+ Second: Consecration to do all the will of God as declared by the Lord Jesus.

+ Third: Recognition of the Holy Spirit as revealer, guide, interpreter, teacher, and empowerer. For without the presence of the Spirit of God in our hearts our consecration would be valueless. We would not be able to live it. And without a knowledge of the teaching of Jesus our consecration would be nonintelligent.

Establishing the Kingdom

The great purpose of Jesus Christ in coming to the world was to establish the kingdom of God. The kingdom of God is universal, containing all moral intelligences willingly subject to the will of God both in heaven and on earth, both angels and men. The kingdom of heaven is Christ's kingdom on the earth, which will eventually merge into the kingdom of God. We read of that merging period in the fifteenth chapter of 1 Corinthians, where it says:

> *Then cometh the end, when he shall have delivered up the kingdom to God, even the Father; when he shall have put down all rule and all authority and power.... And when all things shall be subdued unto him, then shall the Son also himself be subject unto him that put all things under him, that God may be all in all.*
>
> (1 Corinthians 15:24, 28)

Now then, in order to establish a kingdom there must be a basis upon which it is to be founded. When the Revolutionary fathers got together in 1776, they laid down the Declaration of Independence, the principles upon which American government was to be founded. They laid down as one of the first principles this one: "All men are born free and equal"—that every man, by his being born a man, is likewise born on an equality with all others. All men are born free and equal before the law; there is no special privilege.

Next, they considered this as the second principle: that man, because of his birth and his free agency, was entitled to "Life, liberty, and the pursuit of happiness."

Then, they agreed on this third principle: that government rests on the consent of the governed.

These were the underlying principles upon which the government was to rest. There was nothing little about them. They did not discuss the doctrines by which these principles were to be made effective, but they laid down the foundational principles upon which was built the greatest system of human government in the world's history.

Now Jesus likewise, when he came to found His kingdom, first enunciated the principles upon which His government was to rest. The eight Beatitudes, as they are given in His official declaration in His Sermon on the Mount, were the great principles upon which His government was to be founded.

A principle is not a dogma or a doctrine. It is that underlying quality, that fundamental truth, upon which all other things are based. The principles of the kingdom of heaven are those underlying qualities upon which the whole structure of the Christian life rests and the principles upon which the real government of Jesus Christ will be founded and exercised. The eight Beatitudes are the principles of the kingdom, the Sermon on the Mount is the constitution, and the commandments of Jesus are its laws or statutes.

First, the kingdom is established in the hearts of men. The principles of Jesus Christ are settled in our own spirit. We become citizens of the kingdom of heaven. The aggregate citizenship of the kingdom in this present age constitutes the real Church, which is His body. (See Ephesians 1:22–23.) And throughout the Church age the working of the body is to be apparent in demonstrating to the world the practicability and desirability of the kingdom of heaven, that all men may desire the rule of Jesus in the salvation of men.

> The eight Beatitudes are the principles of the kingdom, the Sermon on the Mount is the constitution, and the commandments of Jesus are its laws or statutes.

It is the purpose of Jesus to make the Church, which is His body, His representative in the world. Just as Jesus came to express God the Father to mankind, and Jesus was necessary to God in order that He might give an expression of Himself to the world, so the Church is necessary to Jesus Christ as an expression of Himself to the world.

Now, the first principle that He laid down was this one: *"Blessed are the poor in spirit, for theirs is the kingdom of heaven"* (Matthew 5:3).

Usually we confuse this with the other one, *"Blessed are the meek"* (verse 5), and we have commonly thought of one who is poor in spirit as being a meek, quiet person—possessing the spirit of meekness. But it is much more than that. The thing Jesus urged upon men was to practice what He had done Himself.

Jesus was the King of glory, yet He laid down all His glory. He came to earth and took upon Himself our condition. *"He took not on him the nature of angels; but took on him the seed of Abraham"* (Hebrews 2:16). He took upon Himself the condition of mankind, that is, of human nature's liability to sin. Therefore, He was *"in all points tempted like as we are, yet without sin"* (Hebrews 4:15). And because of the fact that He took upon Himself our nature and understood the temptations that are common to man, He is *"able to succour them that are tempted"* (Hebrews 2:18). He understands. He is a sympathetic Christ. Bless God!

Now see! *"Blessed are the poor in spirit."* Blessed is he who regards the interests of the kingdom of heaven as paramount to every other interest in the world, paramount to his own personal interest. Blessed is he whose interest in life, whose interest in the world is only used to extend the interest of the kingdom of heaven. Blessed is he who has lost his own identity as an individual and has become a citizen of the kingdom. Blessed is he who forgets to hoard wealth for himself, but who uses all he has and all he is for the extension of the kingdom of heaven. It is putting the law of love of God and one another into practice.

So after Jesus had laid down the things that He possessed, then bless God, He was able to say to us, as He had experienced it Himself, *"Blessed are the poor in spirit, for theirs is the kingdom of heaven."*

We commonly think as we read the Word of God that some of the teachings of Jesus were accidental or were applied to a particular individual and no one else. So we think of the rich young ruler, who came to Jesus and said:

> *Good Master, what shall I do to inherit eternal life? And Jesus said unto him.... Thou knowest the commandments, Do not commit*

adultery, Do not kill, Do not steal, Do not bear false witness, Honor thy father and thy mother. And he said, All these have I kept from my youth up.... [Jesus] said unto him, Yet lackest thou one thing: sell all that thou hast, and distribute unto the poor, and thou shalt have treasure in heaven: and come, follow me. (Luke 18:18–22)

Don't you see, Jesus was applying to that young man that first principle of the kingdom. We have said that young man was covetous and he loved his wealth, etc., and that was keeping him out of the kingdom of heaven. Not so. Jesus was applying one of the principles of the kingdom to that young man's life. He turned away sorrowful. He had not developed to the place where he could do that thing.

There is an apocryphal story that tells us that the rich young ruler was Barnabas. After the resurrection and the coming of the Holy Ghost, Barnabas received from heaven the thing Jesus had tried to impart to him. He forgot all about Barnabas, his own interests, and his own desires, and he sold his great possessions and came with the others and laid them at the apostles' feet.[12] *"Blessed are the poor in spirit, for theirs is the kingdom of heaven."* So Jesus was able, after all, to get the real thing in the heart of Barnabas that He desired in the beginning.

The real miracle of the Holy Ghost at Pentecost was not the outward demonstration of tongues, but that it produced such intense unselfishness in the hearts of all baptized that they each sold their lands and estates and parted the money to every man as he had need. They were moved by God into one family. Their brother's interest was equal to their own. That was *"Blessed are the poor in spirit."*

The second principle of the kingdom is this: *"Blessed are they that mourn: for they shall be comforted."* (Matthew 5:4). This figure is taken from the old prophets, who when the nation sinned, took upon themselves the responsibility of the nation. They put sackcloth on their body and ashes on their head and in mourning and tears went down before

---

12. An exact source for this apocryphal story could not be located. The Apocrypha is noncanonical or extrabibilical literature and is not considered inspired by the Holy Spirit. Therefore, the presumption that the rich young ruler was Barnabas is unconfirmed.

God for days and weeks, until the people turned to God. They became the intercessors between God and man and in some instances in the Word we read where God looked and wondered. He wondered that there was no intercessor. There were no mourners who took upon themselves the responsibility of the sins of the people, who dared to stand between man and God.

We see how wonderfully Moses stood between God and the people. When God said to him after they had made the golden calf, *"Let me alone...that I may consume them: and I will make of thee a great nation"* (Exodus 32:10). Moses said, "Not so, Lord. What will the Egyptians say, what will be the effect upon Thy great name? Will they not say that their God destroyed them?" (See Exodus 32:12.)

God had said to Moses, *"I will make of thee a great nation,"* but Moses was big enough to turn aside the greatest honor that God could bestow upon a man—to become the father of a race.

> *And Moses returned unto the Lord, and said, Oh, this people have sinned a great sin, and have made them gods of gold. Yet now, if thou wilt forgive their sin—and if not, blot me, I pray thee, out of thy book.*　　　　　　　　　　　　　　　(verses 31–32)

The prophet became the great intercessor. He took upon himself the burdens and sins of the people, and when he got down to confess he did not say, "Oh! These people are so weak, and they do this and that." But when he got down to pray he would say, "Lord God, we are unworthy." He was one with his people. He was identified with them, as one with them. He was not putting any blame on them. He was big enough to take the whole blame, the entire responsibility, and go down before God and lay the whole matter before God until the blessed mercy of God was again given to the people.

"Blessed are the poor in spirit....Blessed are they that mourn" (Matthew 5:3–4). Blessed is the man who comprehends the purposes of God, who understands his responsibility and possibility, who by God-given mourning and crying, turns the people to God. With his heart yearning for

sinners, he becomes a mourner before God and takes the responsibility of fallen men on his own life. He goes down in tears and repentance before God until men turn to God and the mercy of God is shown to mankind.

In the day that God puts the spirit of mourning upon Pentecost, it will be the gladdest day that heaven ever knew. Blessed be His precious name!

Do you know, it always jars me down in the depths of my spirit when I hear people say hard things about churches and sects. That is not our place. Our place is as intercessor—as the one who is to stand between the living and the dead, as those whom God can trust and use to pray down the power and mercy and blessing of God upon this old race.

First we see that the kingdom is based on principles. Principles are greater than doctrines. Principles are the foundation stones upon which all other things rest. Doctrines are the rules, the details by which we endeavor to carry out the things that the principles contain; but the principles are the great foundation stones upon which all things rest.

Absolute Consecration

Let us turn away from this until we see Jesus at the Jordan, consecrating Himself to His own life work, then we will understand how the Christian is to consecrate himself to carry out the principles.

The Word tells us that when Jesus began to be about thirty years of age, He came down to the River Jordan where John was baptizing and presented Himself for baptism. John looked in amazement on Him and said, *"I have need to be baptized of thee, and comest thou to me?"* But Jesus said, *"Suffer it to be so now; for thus it becometh us to fulfill all righteousness"* (Matthew 3:14–15). Unto *"all righteousness."*

Listen! Hear the declaration to which Jesus Christ was baptized; it was His consecration unto *"all righteousness."* There was no further to go. It comprehends all there is of consecration and commitment unto the will of God and all there is of good. Unto *"all righteousness."* Bless God!

So Jesus understandingly permitted Himself to be baptized of John unto *"all righteousness."* Now listen! You and I have also been baptized. But see! Immediately after He was baptized, something took place. First, the Spirit of God came upon Him as a dove and abode upon Him. (See Matthew 3:16.) Then we read He was led by the Spirit into the wilderness to be tempted of the devil. (See Matthew 4:1.) It was not the devil who led Him into the wilderness. It was the Holy Ghost.

In the sixteenth chapter of Leviticus, we see one of the beautiful figures that will illustrate that to you. On the Day of Atonement, there were brought two goats. The priest laid his hands upon one and put a towrope around its neck; then the Levite took the towrope and led it three days into the barren sands of the wilderness, and left it there to die. (See Leviticus 16:7–22.) That is the picture of the life-death of Jesus Christ.

The Holy Ghost is God's Levite. He put the towrope on the neck of Jesus Christ and led Him likewise three days—a year for a day, God's three days—into the wilderness. What for? To prove out, to test out the real fact of His obedience unto God and whether His consecration was going to stand. So the Spirit, the Holy Ghost, led Jesus into the wilderness.

Now, I want you to see something. We are triune beings just as God Himself is triune. You will see the character of the consecration that Jesus made at the Jordan. God is triune. He is God the Father, God the Son, and God the Holy Ghost. Man is also triune. The Word says,

> *I pray God your whole spirit and soul and body be preserved blameless unto the coming of our Lord Jesus Christ.*
> (1 Thessalonians 5:23)

So, when Jesus went into the wilderness, He encountered a peculiar temptation peculiar to each separate department of His being. The Word of God says He fasted forty days and was hungry. Satan came to Him and said, *"If thou be the Son of God, command that these stones be made bread"* (Matthew 4:3). But Jesus could not do it. If He had done that, He would have been exercising His own authority in His own behalf, and He had committed Himself unto *"all righteousness."* He only lived to express God, He only lived to express the Father. He said, "The words I speak, I speak not of Myself. The work that I do I do not of Myself." (See John 14:10.) All He said and all He did and all He was, was the expression of God the Father.

May the Lord give us an understanding of the utterness of what a real baptismal consecration ought to be. When an individual comes and commits himself to Christ once and for all and forever, he ceases to be, he ceases to live in his own behalf, to live for himself any longer, but becomes the utter expression of Jesus Christ to mankind.

So Satan had no power to tempt a man who had made a consecration like that. The hunger calls of Jesus's body, after He had fasted forty days, were not enough to turn Him aside from the consecration He had made to God.

The second temptation was one peculiar to the mind (soul). He was taken to a pinnacle of the temple, and Satan said, "Do something spectacular; cast yourself down; let the people see You are an unusual person, and that You can do unusual things, and they will give You their acclaim." (See Matthew 4:6.)

Jesus could not do that. There was nothing, bless God, in the mind of Jesus Christ that could tempt Him to be disobedient to the consecration He had made to God, unto *"all righteousness."* So He turned the temptation aside.

The third temptation was one peculiar to the spirit. By a supernatural power Jesus is permitted to see, *"All the kingdoms of the world, and the glory of them,"* in a moment of time. Then Satan said unto Him, *"All these things will I give thee, if thou wilt fall down and worship me"* (Matthew 4:8–9). But Jesus turned him aside. No crossless crowning for the Son of God, no bloodless glory for my Lord. He had come to express God to the world. He had come to demonstrate one thing to you and me. That is, that man relying on God can have the victory over sin and Satan.

Bless God! That is the peculiar thing about the life of Jesus Christ that makes Him dear to your heart and mine.

After going on the towrope of the Holy Ghost for three years as the first goat, through the sorrows and trials and disappointments of life—even ministering and blessing—though the world cursed Him, He was able to come as the second goat and present Himself as the sinless, spotless sacrifice unto God at the cross.

If Jesus had fallen down anywhere along the line, if there had been a single instance where He had failed to express God to the world, He could never have been the Savior of the world. *"He became the author of eternal salvation"* (Hebrews 5:9). He was honored of God in being permitted to die for mankind, having triumphed, having presented Himself the sinless, spotless sacrifice unto God. His blood flowed for all the race. Blessed be His name!

We have seen two things. We have seen the principles of Jesus Christ. We have seen His consecration to carry out those principles. He consecrated Himself utterly unto the mind and will of God. But now we are going a step farther.

Even unto Death

We come to the last night of the Lord's life. He is with His disciples in the upper room. Here comes the final act, the consummation of all His life. There is a phase of this act that I know the Lord has made clear to many.

They sat around the table after they had eaten their supper, Jesus took bread and broke it, saying, *"Take, eat: this is my body, which is broken for you"* (see Matthew 26:26; 1 Corinthians 11:24), and yet He was there in the flesh.

Now, what did it mean? What was its significance? This: by that act the Lord Jesus Christ pledged Himself before God, before the holy angels, before men, that He would not stop short of dying for the world. There was no limit. He was faithful *"even unto death"* (Matthew 26:38).

Just as He had been faithful in life and had lived each day the conscious life-death, dying to every desire of His mind and will and being, He is now going one step further. He is going to be faithful *"even unto death."*

So He said, "Take and eat, this is My body, broken for you." After supper likewise, He took the cup, when He had drunk, saying, *"My blood of the new testament"* (Matthew 26:28).

Now you listen. From time immemorial mankind has been in the habit of pledging themselves in the cup. There is no date that mankind has of its origin. It is so ancient we do not know when the custom began, when men began to pledge themselves in the wine cup, but our Jesus sanctified the custom to God and His Church forever.

Jesus poured the wine into the cup, took it, and said, *"This is my blood of the new testament,"* and He drank that Himself. That was the pledge of the Lord Jesus Christ. Having laid down the principles of the gospel of the Son of God, having walked and lived and suffered for three years, now He was going to the very uttermost. There was no further to go. He said, *"This is my blood of the new testament,"* meaning He would give His life for the world.

That is not all. That was His pledge, but after He had drunk, saying, *"Drink ye all of it"* (Matthew 26:27). And when they took the cup of which their Lord had drunk, they drank to that pledge. They were made partakers in the same pledge and likewise pledged themselves, *"My blood of the new testament."* Bless God.

Christianity had character in it. Jesus Christ put character in it. Bless God! *"My blood of the new testament."* The other day I was going over the list of the apostles as they are given by Hippolytus, one of the early writers, and he tells us that five of the twelve were crucified just as Jesus was. Others died by the spear and sword, and three died natural deaths after enduring tortures. So it meant for them just what it means for their Lord, *"My blood of the new testament."* We see the degree of faithfulness to which they pledged themselves that night.

We have loved and admired the spirit of the apostles. The spirit of Jesus Christ was so intense in the early Christians, that millions of them gave their lives for the Son of God; multitudes of whom died the death of martyrs and multitudes died in the war to exterminate Christianity. Thirty million! Think of that. It gives some meaning to the saying that "The blood of the martyrs was the seed of the church."

How often have you and I taken the Lord's cup? Has it meant that to you and me, and does it mean that to you and me now? Beloved, I have no doubt that the sacred cup has touched many lips, perhaps the lips of most of you. If we have been understanding, comprehending Christians, we have realized it meant to us just what it did to the Lord— our everlasting pledge of faithfulness.

There is no place for sin in the Christian's life. There is no place for letting down in the Christian's life. There is no place for weakening in the Christian's life. Paul said, when they were having a hard time, "*Ye have not yet resisted unto blood, striving against sin*" (Hebrews 12:4). That was expected of them. They were expected to resist even unto death; so Paul said, "*Ye have not yet resisted unto blood.*" In the Revelation, the Church in Smyrna is commanded, "*Be thou faithful unto death, and I will give thee a crown of life*" (Revelation 2:10).

In this land, after our fathers had signed the old Declaration of Independence they pledged, "Our lives, our fortunes, and our sacred honor," then they went out and gave themselves to eight years of war in order to make it good.

When people make a declaration on principles, it is going to cost them something and it costs them something. After awhile the men in the old Revolutionary Army got where they did not have shoes on their feet, but in the depth of winter they tied straw and rags on their feet. They had stood by principles, they had lived by principles, they were ready to die by principles, and the British tracked them by the blood marks on the snow.

So Jesus Christ, in enlisting an army, put them under a kindred pledge with Himself. He pledged Christians on the same plane with Himself. Just as far as the Lord went, they went "even unto death."

The real purpose of becoming a Christian is not to save yourself from hell or to be saved to go to heaven. It is to become a child of God with the character of Jesus Christ, to stand before men pledged unto the uttermost—*"even unto death"*—by refusing to sin, refusing to bow your head in shame. Preferring to die rather than dishonor the Son of God.

If the character of Jesus Christ has entered into you and into me, then it has made us like the Christ. It has made us like Him in purpose. It has made us like Him in fact. Bless God! His Spirit is imparted to us. Bless God for that same unquenchable fidelity that characterized the Son of God.

> *Be thou faithful unto death, and I will give thee a crown of life.*
> (Revelation 2:10)

Consecration Prayer

My God and Father,

In Jesus's name I come to Thee, take me as I am. Make me what I ought to be in spirit, in soul, in body. Give me power to do right. If I have wronged any to confess, to repent, to restore—no matter what it costs. Wash me in the blood of Jesus that I may now become Thy child and manifest Thee in a perfect spirit, a holy mind, a sickless body, to the glory of God. Amen.

22

MY CONSECRATION AS A CHRISTIAN

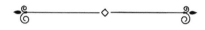

I, this day, consecrate my entire life to glorify my heavenly Father by my obedience to the principles of Jesus Christ through the power of the Holy Spirit. All my effort from now on will be directed in an effort to demonstrate the righteousness of God in whatever I may be engaged.

Principle 1

All earthly things that I possess shall not be considered my own, but belonging to my heavenly Father, and shall be held in trust by me to be used and directed by the wisdom of the Spirit of God, as the law of loving people as Christ loved them may dictate.

If at any time God should raise up men wiser than myself, I will gladly commit my all to their use and turn over all my possessions to them for distribution.

If at any time in my life I should be engaged in any earthly business and should employ people to aid me in conducting it, I shall reward them justly and equally, comparing their own energy expended with my own after adding a sufficient amount to my own to cover all risk that may be involved in the operation of my business.

I shall consider my employees my equals with rights to the blessings of nature and life equal to my own. I shall not strive to elevate myself to a position of comfort above the rest of my employees and shall direct all my efforts to bring all mankind to an equal plane, where all enjoy the comforts of life and fellowship together.

Principle 2

I shall not cease to cry to God and implore Him to deliver mankind from the effects of sin, as long as sin lasts, but shall cooperate with God in the redemption of mankind.

I will have seasons of prayer and fasting in behalf of mankind, weeping and bewailing their lost condition and imploring God to grant them repentance unto life as the Spirit of God may lead me.

Principle 3

I shall live my life in meekness, never defending my own personal rights, but shall leave all judgment in God who judges righteously and rewards all according to their works.

I shall not render evil for evil or railing for railing, but shall bless all and do good to enemies to return for evil.

By God's grace I shall keep all hardness and harshness out of my life and actions; rather I shall be gentle and unassuming, not professing above what God has imported to me nor lifting myself above my brethren.

Principle 4

I shall consider righteous acts as more necessary to life and happiness than food and drink, and not let myself be bribed or coerced into any unrighteous action for any earthly consideration.

Principle 5

By God's grace, I will always be merciful, forgiving those who have transgressed against me and endeavoring to correct the ills of humanity instead of merely punishing them for their sins.

Principle 6

I shall not harbor any impure thoughts in my mind but shall endeavor to make my every act uplifting.

I shall regard my procreative organs sacred and holy and never use them for any purpose other than that which God created them for.

I shall regard the home as sacred and always guard my actions in the presence of the opposite sex, so as not to cause a man and his wife to break their vows to one another. I shall be chaste with the opposite sex who are married, considering them as sisters. I shall be careful not to cause them undue pain by playing on their affections.

Principle 7

I will always strive to be a peacemaker, first, by being peaceful myself and avoiding all unfruitful contentions. I shall treat all with justice and regard their rights and their free agency, never trying to force any to my point of view.

If I should offend anyone knowingly, I shall immediately apologize.

I will not scatter evil reports about any person and so try to defame their character, or repeat things that I am not certain of being true.

I will strive to remove the curse of strife among brethren by acting as a peacemaker.

Principle 8

I shall not become discouraged when I am persecuted on account of the righteousness mentioned above nor murmur on account of any suffering I undergo, but shall gladly give my life rather than depart from this high standard of life, rejoicing because I know I have a great reward in heaven.

I shall strive to make the above principles the ideal of all the world and give my life and energy to see mankind get the power from God to practice the same.

—John G. Lake

ABOUT THE COMPILER
ROBERTS LIARDON

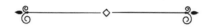

Born in Tulsa, Oklahoma, Roberts Liardon is a leading Protestant church historian. He founded Roberts Liardon Ministries, along with Embassy Christian Center, Embassy Ministerial Association, Spirit Life Bible College, and Operation 500. He also founded the Reformers and Revivalists Historical Museum. At seventeen, Liardon published his first book, *I Saw Heaven*, which sold over 1.5 million copies and catapulted him into the public eye. To date, Liardon's books, including the God's Generals series, have sold over 15 million copies worldwide and have been translated into more than 60 languages. Liardon's DVD series *God's Generals* became one of the bestselling Christian DVD series in history. Having ministered in over 125 countries to members of the public and to world leaders, Liardon is also recognized internationally. In addition to being an author and a church historian, he is a public speaker, a spiritual leader, and a humanitarian. Liardon continues to manage and expand his international headquarters in Sarasota, Florida, and his office in London, England.

Welcome to Our House!

We Have a Special Gift for You

It is our privilege and pleasure to share in your love of Christian books. We are committed to bringing you authors and books that feed, challenge, and enrich your faith.

To show our appreciation, we invite you to sign up to receive a specially selected **Reader Appreciation Gift**, with our compliments. Just go to the Web address at the bottom of this page.

God bless you as you seek a deeper walk with Him!

WE HAVE A GIFT FOR YOU. VISIT:

whpub.me/nonfictionthx

WHITAKER
HOUSE